WHO ARE YOU
Wonderland and Places to trick Soul

DR MIA MORGAN WHITE

ISBN:

LCCN: 2018912054 ISBN-13: 978-0-9703419-4-5

DEDICATION

For all of us
How to survive humans

ACKNOWLEDGMENTS

Thank the Sun for shining and Stars and Light for Helping

Spiritual Keys to Wonderland and Places to trick Soul

My book, this book, WHO ARE YOU was born out of my two big things. My parents never teaching me about racism and my town conspiring to do the same. I grew up in the city of Oakland, but my parents decided if none of the children in our family knew racism existed on the planet, our subconscious would not act accordingly. So, it wouldn't be full of all the trash that cruelty based on class restrictions does to all humans and without any sexism would also do the same. So I only learned the kind things in the world...buam, baum, baum you know some villains were very happy-as this Alice entered into some wonder lands. So, as a doctor who specializes in the brain and as someone who was born with so many spiritual gifts, one thing I know is we are all Soul. The other thing I know is we all have a purpose, and some people don't realize that every ism is set aside to keep us from our purpose.

So, when we look at Asian hate crimes, right now, we're spending a lot of time with the structure crumbling, the structure in which we're taught hate this person, don't hate that person. This person hates you, that person hates you, and all the permissions to be evil. So, I knew as a little girl that slavery happened, and my parents taught me about slavery because of the book Roots and the movie Roots, but they also taught me about the Holocaust and the book The Diary of Anne Frank and the movie The Diary of Anne Frank. They did not fill anything in in-between those years or between the years in which they'd been written or produced as movies the time I grew up. So, what they taught me, I'll explain to you in the next chapter, but it's basically what happens when you don't teach hate and then you are a member of Mensa® like I am with such a high IQ.

People like me, We're not even just members of Mensa®. We're called the 99s because our IQ is 99.9999999, the highest of the population. So, Mensa® is a society of geniuses that are the top 2% of the brains in the world. Now I always say, if anyone can say that to you without this correction, maybe check their Mensa® card because it would have to be the 2% of the top brains in the tested world or the tested brains in the world because we didn't test everyone on this planet. So, the math would be off with 2% because not everyone in the world was tested. But we are the top 2% of the brains and the tested world which means almost every human, because every test you take in school or a doctor's office, therapists, psychologists, sociologists, educational studies, any of those types of tests are testing IQ. I LOVE TeaParties.

They told me in elementary school, I was a 99. I was like Bart Simpson getting in trouble all the time. I mean, not too frequently because my mother brought cupcakes to the school and she would in the middle of her workday come and peek in the classroom windows or volunteer to help grade papers or help with the kids. She always went with us on field trips. She would take off work to go with us on field trips. So, the women in my family are raised like perfect housewives, like perfect Stepford wives, and the only reason I say that it's an honor to them because they're beautiful. The women in my family always dressed beautifully. They act beautifully. They raised their children wonderfully and perfectly and they treat their husbands like they are gods that are adored and worshiped even sometimes to a fault if the husband's not really such a nice guy. I do have one cousin who has always acted like a demon so I've always since I was little called her TAZ.

My family has a rule that I broke, and the rule is you don't get married to get divorced, which means no matter what your husband does, no matter who he is towards you or children or the world you are not supposed to get a divorce. Once you get married, you just stay. If you're abused, you get abused. If your kids are raped, they get raped, and it comes from our bloodline. It comes from our cultural heritage and so it's just a belief that divorce is not an option and in the area come from ore families and friends with 54 years, 60 years, 70-year happy marriages with, of course, you know, the three horrible sprinkled in there, but the rule applied to everyone.

When you have a genius mind, you see the world differently. Not just the setup by my parents, my church, and our town not to have any of us understand any cruelty based on class restrictions, meaning teaching us no stereotypes. So, whatever race you are, my family, my parent, my church, our school, everybody around us only taught us the good stuff about every person's race and they didn't turn it into stereotypes about that race. As a child, I didn't have dolls that looked like me. I had dolls that look like everyone, but they weren't playing together like one big kumbaya because as a 99, we're at the top of 1% of that 2% of brains in the world. So, you can BS us, but only if it's something we can't scientifically test. So, you could be evil and if we haven't decided to study or look into evil we may not see your motives, but as you behave, everything we do study is going to show us what to do and how to beat you miserably.

When I say that, I mean, like as a profiler. I realized that I could use the skills that I have in reprogramming human brains to also be an excellent profiler and figure out the brain, the personality, the spirituality, the psychology, sociology, philosophy, and underlying motives of the person who may have committed a crime. So, I always joke that when I come in as a profiler, they don't know the crime. They don't know what was taken in the field I work in. I consult for a lawyer sometimes, but not too often. Usually, there's a crime where I feel like it hurt old people or children and I will come in and take that crime and I always say, they show me a vase with some water, not literally but figuratively. They don't know what happened and they don't know who did it. So, there's a vase and water and I have to figure out what was in the vase and who took it and where they are and how they can be caught.

So, I started writing comic books because I had been writing self-help books and travel books for over a decade. Then I love comic books because I grew up with mythology and I grew up with heroes and I grew up with superheroes and I grew up going to the museum and the opera and plays and musical theater. Classical music is my favorite music and so opera does two things. My favorite things, costumes and classical music. Yes. With the great stories. So, when I walk through the world, I don't see the world you see. I don't see it because of my personality. I'm very quirky and I'm very witty and I'm very pretty. So, I decided that each part of me would host the best parts of the world that we have to encounter.

So, it's like, if there's something terrible, I'm extremely witty and logical about it so that we can work our way through any traumas, and then I'm very spiritual, spiritually gifted, seeing and hearing the spiritual worlds. I was born that way and then I studied books and learned about it. I went to schools like Xavier's School X-Men and then I trained my skills, honed my skills. As I write my books it helps people heal and be inspired but also it helps us maybe have a little bit of the gifts that I was born with so that when you walk through the world, you don't only see it through the programming that was put there to destroy you.

So, the reason I decided to write a nice way to talk about racism is, because as long as we talk about it in the lower realms, meaning the way someone wants you to view the world. So, you think it's a hopeless, terrible, bad place, or they want you to be a hopeless, terrible, bad person. Then you're missing the bigger game, the true game, what all of that was really about, gain. Because my parents and my family and my church and my school didn't teach any of that and I was raised in the church. I studied in college and treated it like Sherlock Holmes or Agatha Christie, like a terrible mystery, a terrible crime has been committed against souls to make them think they're not souls. They're going around acting like AI puppets, or even old-school marionette puppets in a video game and that video game is earth.

So, as we look into our next chapter, then I want you to think, how could they have made a person like me in a world full of people, unlike me. And no one else was able to break or change that programming, meaning my programming. They taught me what is evil and they taught me what is good. So, they didn't say, oh, you should love Chinese people, or you should love Korean people. They took me to tea gardens and taught me so many things about the world. I love studying botany. I love tea. I love gardening and I love parties like nobody's business. I love parties. I don't drink. I don't smoke. I don't gamble. I don't cheat. There are so many things I don't do. Party Do. Your party may be different than a party to me, but don't get confused when I say party because I mean, wild, crazy parties like should be on a movie.

They are so unbelievably wild and the things that are happening are so extreme and all the ways too partying with cowboys and it's just people standing around talking and listening to good music. But I mean, parties with costumes and fireworks and people spinning from ceilings. But my family and my town and my city gave me programming that I share with my clients as a joy coach, as a matchmaker for millionaires and multi-millionaires/billionaires so they can have happy lives. I was given dolls. So, they didn't say somebody hates these people or we have been at war with those people. They just gave me a doll of a geisha and I loved her. She was so pretty and before they gave me ones I could hold. I stared for hours at ones in our homes in cases.

My grandmother and my mother had dolls from my grandfather, having been career Navy, he would bring things home. So, I knew the beautifully carved furniture that I loved had been made by these same people or my mom would take me to Chinatown as a child to shop and I'd get my favorite foods, my favorite cookies because I'm not really big on sweets, but I love fortune cookies so much I should own a factory. Now as a member of Mensa®, that meant, I also had to figure out how fortune cookies are made and what's their history. But that's another Mensa® tip... Now is the time to understand what it means is: it doesn't mean we're better than you. It doesn't mean we're smarter than you. It means genius minds, process information differently and seek information differently with extreme fervor.

So, once I decide I like something or there's something that I don't know that I'm interested in knowing then I have to learn everything about it and then master it. Once I master it, my brain just wants to learn something new and go onto the next thing and we compile it and there's this balance. I'm a Libra and so there's this Libran balance of learning everything about something, mastering that thing, keeping the things that are important while at the same time, knowing as a doctor to dump the things that aren't important. Well, I figured that out as a teenager. I was 12 years old when I figured out do not store unnecessary information in my brain cells.

But I also learned that I have the ability to record history visually in my mind. So, I can tell you what I wore to Disneyland when I was four. What that outfit was, what happened, what I did. So, my mom used to take us to

Disneyland every year, and one time I say it this way now, but I'll say it to you the way she would like it said first. So, one time in Disneyland, I was 4 and lost, and I did every social protocol my mom taught me. I found an authority. She always taught me to trust authority. She taught me the police are the knights of the time period. So, first, she taught me mythology. I love the Renaissance. I love Shakespeare (an obsession she was not counting on). So, she taught me to relate the current police, not our current police this year, but of my childhood to always view police as the knights, because she knew I understood knights and then relate that to in this time period, the world would be worse without them. Not that every one of them was good because not every person is good. So, that's the way she would have explained it to you and that's the way she explained it to me.

Now, when I say every social protocol, she taught me what to do if I was lost. Do you know that woman literally watched me being lost and took pictures and then later on, of course, they found her because SHE was not missing because she was there to take the pictures? She was able to take pictures, (which later appeared in my baby book) it was not her purpose to take pictures she just thought I was so cute once she found me. I explained to her, when I was like 18 and I said, mother, do you understand that I could have had trauma? Stress wasn't a word in my life. So, that comes from dumping unnecessary stuff. But we'll get into that in the next chapter or the fourth chapter. But pretty much I wanted my mother to understand. She thought it was delightful that I went up to the authority. I introduced myself. I didn't cry. I wasn't like that crying kid that was lost. I was her logical little genius baby that she'd always say, "you're smarter than the average bear" and I would say, "make the world a better place".

If God gives you spiritual gifts and mental gifts, it's your job. If God makes you beautiful, it's your job to make the world a better place. So, I just went, and I introduced myself. First I figured out who was the person in authority. They're usually wearing some form of uniform. Once I assessed that --she had photos of all of this. Then once I figured out the person in authority, I kindly introduced myself. I asked their name, I put my little hand out. I shook their hand and then I informed them that I had misplaced my mother and I was lost, and I needed help finding her. She had photos of all of these stages as well. So, when I was 18 and I realized that these photos meant I was only in my mind lost! because that woman knew where I was the whole time. Otherwise, how did she take the pictures?

So, I told her mother, I could have had really a traumatic moment. Those memories could be locked in as trauma because I didn't know she was there taking the photos. I didn't know anyone knew where I was. She said, but Mia, it was so cute. It was so cute that you went up. It was so cute that you did everything you were taught to do, and you got yourself, the help that you needed. Then I realized, I never cried. Little kids cry. What the heck is wrong with me. I was just like; I'm just not built that way. So, it was very cute and so I just forgave her, as I do with everyone. AND I was like, at any moment, you could have ended that. She was like, well, yes, but you were okay, and I was like, I wasn't okay. I was lost until you were found. Then she laughed because my mom was like such a crazy narcissist. She was so controlling and just so wild, but she always said it's to protect you. Right. No. It's because I'm keeping you safe. But I didn't know about narcissists for another 20 years after that.

So, it was very interesting. Two perspectives of the same human, one deciding these moments could continue for her pride and her enjoyment and the pictures were so cute to watch me walk up, watch me, wait my turn to speak with the person, the officer, to help me. Walk up, shake his hand, introduce myself. You see me: (picture 1) talking to him after I wait my turn and I waited so patiently with my little hands behind my back. Then I went and then I lift (photo 2) my little head and I talked to them and then there's another picture of me reaching down and shaking his hand and him shaking my hand. Then there's another one where we're discussing the problem and finding a solution.

Well, we can treat life that way but what if we don't have the ability to do, it's rare the human that can reprogram the subconscious of another human. That's what I do for a living. Since I was 21.

Now, programming a human is quite easy. We all do it by accident. Billboards, friend circles, school groups. We tell each other stereotypes. Gossips use whatever pops into their heads as logic and truth and state it to other humans and harm people's souls every day of the world. But there's this really old philosophy and I'll kind of end this chapter with it: wherein great minds discuss hopes and dreams. Things that aren't in the world yet that they want to make manifest or actualize in the world. Then average minds discuss events that would be people talking about the football game, the weather, the most popular TV show, whatever's on the news, whatever they're being told to talk about.

Without their knowing something just wants them to talk about that so that they never talk about things that would change their lives.

Then small minds discuss people so that would be the gossips, the haters, the trolls. When I say haters, haters and gossips do the same thing. Gossips sometimes think that's normal; their behavior is normal. It's entertaining. It's what we do at church. It's what we do as a town. It's what we do as people because their programming is that they're surrounded by people that that's their form of entertainment. But then when you look at the people that discuss the common events, the average minds. The average minds have the nerve to think they're better off than the small minds. But in truth, the average minds are more controlled in a gladiator level of subconscious mind control of Souls body.

Now I want you to understand what that phrase means, and I don't want to assume what you understand or don't understand. But since this is a book and a course, I would like people to know that average minds are taught they know everything. Now, it differs. What they teach you is everything to know differs by social class, geography, race, gender, age. So, your neighborhood, your state, your city, your house, your school, your income level, your level of beauty, your weight, your height, all of those things are taken into account when teaching you your world. So, you can encounter a kid from another state with all of your same circumstances and their programming will differ like a little turn of a dial on a clock.

You guys are close so you'll be at 11:50 o'clock, they will be at 12 o'clock very close. Got it, but different race, but same everything else might be at three o'clock because they've taught that many things different on a subconscious level.

Billboards, television shows, friends, things you hear grownups talk about, magazines you encounter, as opposed to all the magazines that exist in the world. What books? Are you taught fairytales? Are you not taught fairytales? What stories are you taught? What are you not taught? All of these things program us and none of them announce that they are doing that. So, our belief systems are built on lies, lies attached to programming. So, now you take a kid that doesn't look like those other three kids but is tall, beautiful, athletic, smart, and rich. That kid is going to be at six o'clock and throughout the world all the other kids who look like that and have those same qualifications or have those same quantifiers will also be at six o'clock because the higher you go in; you've got the best of this or that the programming narrows. There are less stereotypes taught to you.

The stereotypes taught to you are about you and then every body else is that everybody else. Got it. You're not taught little things whereas the gossips, their world is as big as that which they gossip about. So, there has been royalty that were gossips and there are, of course, church mothers that are gossips. They gossip about different things, but gossiping is the same thing, it is all evil, usually by someone who envies somebody, and Shakespeare taught us gossip is normally started by someone who envies your life and wants to destroy it. There are, depending on a scholarly opinion, four to six of Shakespeare's plays are built around gossip. Now the higher-level scholars believe that all of Shakespeare plays came from news stories but the tabloid level, which would be the gossip of the time period, that all of the play's characters come from that, especially the tragedies whereas most people would think it's the histories because the histories are real people. But the love stories and the tragedies and the comedies were things that happen in his time or histories before his time or circumstances.

So, what I have taught people my entire career is that Shakespeare, William Shakespeare, works,. his writings, and his intent teach us about every soul we will ever meet, every type of soul we will ever meet. But if you want to create one set of people who get shot by another set of people and everybody looks the other way or does nothing or thinks that's just the way it is. You have to program those people. One set is programmed at seven o'clock and one set is programmed at one o'clock. Got it. So that they're across from each other, but they are taught completely different programming, and their programming clashes. The rationalization of one group for their behavior and the rationalization of the other group for their own behavior and that their behaviors are so different and their programming of what's acceptable behavior. They both cause harm, but one has the legal system behind them and the other does not.

So, as we pare down racism into it was to keep all poor classes battling at all times. That's from caveman days till now. It started with people who all look like each other, wherever you were. Wherever you were in the world, that behavior, and what's acceptable to do to harm others because they are the other didn't originate with same nationality and what somebody looked like, did like, believed, or behaved differently than you. It was just being the other.

So, they looked alike, they looked exactly alike, but they were not your clan. So long before we interacted as continents, long before Soul took on bodies that differed so visually these behaviors took place in everybody meaning the separate word every body, as well as the compound word everybody. Every separate word body. So, every human's body as well as everybody the word together, the compound word meaning all of us as humans, all of us.

So, the all of us and the bodies of each of us were taught and programmed to hate or fear or a combination thereof and envy the other. Then we had permissions to harm the other. So, the poor envied the rich, because the rich had money and food. The rich envied the poor because the poor had peace and happiness. These dynamics of the one and seven continue. Now the one and seven is about hate and hate crimes. But if you do two and eight that's too far apart because all the rest of it works at two and six, two o'clock and six o'clock. Where are the hands at two o'clock and six o'clock? Or if you put the little hand on two and the big hand on six, that's the level of difference. That's where most racism rests not in the shocking hate crimes, like the Holocaust or I always call that when God cried. I was a little kid, and I just would say, God, must have cried because I didn't know about racism, not that it existed at all. I was taught to love every race of people, taught only the best of each culture's history.

I didn't even know that existed on the planet, but I knew the Holocaust took place and I was like, something made us and we're like little ants playing in the ant farm and God already put everything we play with. It just takes us time to open up our consciousness, remember we are Soul, and use that creative flow to say everything that we used to make plastic already existed when dinosaurs existed, but we didn't know how to make plastic because we were using our brainpower to stay alive from animals and elements and starvation. But the human dynamics developed from that period till now the biggest people went out and hunted. Sometimes they returned from the hunt. Sometimes they didn't. We became the biggest predator on the planet because we had to figure out how to kill the biggest predator so we could eat them, the animals.

So, once we became conniving and cunning. Conniving is figuring out how to do something with ill intent or the intent to harm kill or maim and cunning is using your wit to survive or get out of situations. So, if we use the princesses and I promise, you know, I love the princesses, but I'll only use them once or twice in this book. If I slip, please forgive me. Snow White is cunning because she has to figure out how to survive the queen but she's not conniving because she's innocent and loving and kind. She's not trying to figure out how to beat the queen. She's just trying to figure out how to not die. So, she doesn't really fit the definition of cunning or conniving. Little Red Riding hood on the other hand is cunning because she's trying to figure out how to survive, protect her grandmother and defeat the Wolf but she's not conniving. Now in Snow White, the Evil Queen is conniving because she's trying to wiggle her way into the King's life, using spells, using sex, lying, and using people like they're on a chessboard to manipulate the surrounding so she can have the King. Even though she wins that through black magic and hate and all kinds of manipulation, she's conniving enough to then try to kill Snow out of envy. Do you see? So, that's the difference between those words.

So, when we're dealing with racism, there are people who are conniving enough to convince you that racism is about race when racism is about money and racism is about wealth, power, destruction. Racism is about class keeping all the poor as Other. So, you can stay down there and destroy each other in addition to the bigger picture is always about Soul because none of us are human. We are all Soul and racism keeps you at the numbers far enough apart at the one and the seven, so you always got your eye on each other. So that as Soul, you never remember you're Soul, you're too busy being human and figuring out who hates you, who you hate back, who doesn't hate you, but who's beneath you and you hate that you can rob them, you can steal them or from them. That was not a mistake, steal humans then you can steal from them 400 years later and 500 years later, and 600 years later. You steal their ideas; you steal their hope. You steal their children, you steal their lives, and something evil convinced you to let itself live inside you.

Yes, instead of you being Soul and achieving your road, you're a vessel for hate. There's a reason. why the masses experience more racism. It's because it was a game built for the masses. So, you destroy each other, and then the wealthy have it built

So, I would say, take that gumball. Now the paper, the paper, I would wrap higher energy because I don't want that gumball coming back, and I don't want that gumball harming me or anybody else. So, now just decide what you want. The paper is whatever you worship God, Allah, Buddha, Krishna, Sudama, the Lord, the Lady, all that is, is the fates, the Fae, whatever it is that you love and worship. You are a soul, you have the right, you have free will to worship whatever you want, and you use that, and you wrap that and let that be the paper around that gumball that you no longer want to be.

If you have to do this many times a day and change yourself, great. I used to say that when I would go to church conferences or I'd be teaching meditation, I was like, I'm going to be new five times today. I'm going to be new so many times. Every time I go to a workshop I'm coming out new, and I'm going to change five or six times while I'm in there. Keep being my better self, my better self, my better self. People would actually try to hit me with negative energy out of envy. What the heck? How dare you. I want all that hate put in your gumball not mine! life.

You Always learn how to beat Villains by watching anime and reading comic books
Fushigi no Kuni no Arisu

Tony Cheung and Jennifer are examples of Evil fully taking over the human body like the red king and queen …

Tony and Jennifer Cheung stole $193,000 to 220,000.00 from me and these are people who are so hateful to so many races of people. They sit on 7th Street and Harrison in Oakland in front of New Tin's Market (they own this store) every day. Every day, they're there all day saying stuff and they have different racism for all people. They hate white people, and they will say things like we're more racist than white people. We just are taught culturally to keep our mouths shut and let White People take the blame. So, we can get away with more racism. This is Tony and Jennifer Cheung's conscious mind, not just their subconscious hate. That's their conscious Beings, just purely evil and then they'll scratch under their armpits and be like, oh, black people monkey, you monkeys, black people monkey. They don't care even though they have black customers, even though they have white customers because who they are is Evil.

SOULS WHO LET THIS LEVEL OF HATE BECOME WHO THEY ARE - BECOME DEMONS

-Line pushers doing something in violation of physical and spiritual laws daily without regard for following laws of cities.

So, sometimes we get confused in who we are because somebody comes in and tries to redefine you as the thing they hate and get to abuse or rob or cast spells on or send negative energy to and you don't know how many witches who don't violate your meridians but have cast spells to stop pedophiles. So, we're not here to judge people for their magical practices. We're here to help you understand there's a nice way to talk about racism. So, when you look at that, are those humans in Tony and Jennifer Cheung's bodies. Are they human sitting there? They surpassed humans. They're just full-on evil, wearing human flesh costumes.

Now, in the next chapter, we're all wearing human flesh costumes, but you have to make sure what's inside is not pure hate evil, and demonic like Tony and Jennifer Cheung. They have a store called New Tin's Market and it sits at, I think maybe 310 is the address. It's the corner of the tunnel that goes to Oakland, California from Alameda, California. So, when you're in Oakland, California at 7th and Harrison, there's a tunnel that leaves Alameda and goes into Oakland. That's where their store sits and it's a block from the, where you go from Webster and 7th which the tunnel is heading the other way. You're going from Oakland into Alameda and so it sits right there on 7th Street in Oakland. Spewing hate, casting spells, stealing money and laughing about it, bragging about their ability to do it harming White, Black and Mexican People.

What did the state of California say? There are some areas where cultural groups are not pursued that literally rob, countries or states let alone states of Being Each day. And the state of California can't figure out how to stop it. Now we know that if this was a different group and a different social class, compliance officers would go in.

It's like, you're not better at math you're just stealing. You're conniving, you're evil. So, you don't have money because you're better at math. You don't have money because you are better at making money. You're not better than white people at business. You're better because the state doesn't shoot you for walking down the street on a sunny day because police don't attack you. The people that are supposed to make you pay things like taxes, mortgages, pay for the city ordinances , pay building permits, pay for contractor licenses, you ignore all that and don't do it and just be an illegal contractor. Don't pay your sales tax, lie about your income, take everything in cash. There are certain things we have in a society where certain races of people do that and then have this superiority to their level of evil wherein and say they are better at business, they will say we hate white people we get to do what we want and then they'll say we're more racist than white people.

The way I was brought up I didn't know any of that existed and then studying in university, what racism is and how it works and how classism works and how sexism works that's a delusional level of evil that is nothing but demonic because, see, it's never been any of all white person. We've never had a period in history where every white person was racist, and we never will. So, for them, Tony Cheung, Jennifer Cheung, Wakako Uritani in ChinaTown Oakland to say things like that about white people is appalling. How dare those three people be so racist? How dare they be so demonic? But that is what their soul is. That's what's inside their human flesh costume assuming darkness. So, this chapter is about what's inside your human flesh costume. Is anger inside of it? Is fear inside of it? Is pain inside of it? Are traumas inside of it? Are undealt with memories of this lifetime and other lifetimes inside of it? My sister growing up, I have more than one sister, but we came in pairs literally. So, I have two sisters that are older than I am, who were from a different wife in another state then I have the sister I grew up with, and then as we grew up and we were teenagers, we got two new little baby sisters.

So, it's like, we all grew up in sets of two, even though there are six of us. Actually, there's a seventh because when those two grew up when they were grown women old enough to have kids, a new baby came but my Dad died. So, the sister I grew up with was definitely afraid of water and even though I was a little kid, I knew that she must have lived a past life. I was raised in the church. I was raised in the Baptist church and Catholic church where nobody believes in the reincarnation of anyone except for Jesus.

But one thing I knew is God gave me 8 spiritual gifts. So, I knew that reincarnation was real, but I also knew that I was soul, and I knew everybody else was soul. So, I knew that my sister would be crying when she had to get her hair washed or when the water got on her face because she must've died that way and it was still stuck in her. So, when I first started doing Energetic Anatomy therapy for people, I had already been practicing Chinese Medicine for a very long time and I had mastered it. Remember that little Mensa®® thing where we learn it, we master it. So, I don't care if it's painting or sewing. Whatever we learn our brain forces us to learn everything about that and master that and then we master that, and we can learn like five or eleven things at once. But one thing we don't do is engage things that don't help peoples' lives be better, has no value and I mean, logical value.

I wrote courses to change the way we think about our actions in Visions For Our Lives.

Our brain assessed this is not going to help us help the world or this is a thing that is invalid. I would consider football more valid to me than baseball because there was a time where I dated football players and when you date football players, they want you to understand what's going on. Whereas my mom loved baseball and when I would go to the A's game, I would take stationary. That's this beautiful paper for those of you who only have texts throughout your life. There's this stuff called paper and then a lot of people spent 800 years of human history making papers beautiful because we would write on it to have conversations and correspond with each other.

So, I would take lovely stationery and nail polish, and I would paint my nails and as my nails dried, I would write letters to friends during the baseball game, professional baseball games, sitting next to my mother who wanted me there because she loves baseball and wanted to share that with me. But she knew, I found it exceedingly boring, extremely boring, painfully and punishable. I felt like I was on punishment at a baseball game, so boring to me, but I knew it was exciting to everyone but me.

So, I would go with my mother and I would take my things and she would not complain that I wrote letters because she knew there was so much brainpower not being used while I sat there and watched the world's longest, most boring game. Baseball is extremely exciting. Now, if they could just cut all the parts out of the middle and just the exciting parts that happen, like once every half hour to 45 minutes to an hour, then it would be good. But then that part is only about eight to 10 minutes of four hours out of your life and it's sporadic and you don't know when it's really coming and if you're not paying attention, you can miss it, which is kind of ridiculous and frustrating when you think of it. You could sit there for an hour watching, watching, watching, and then turn to get a hot dog or go to the bathroom and miss that one exciting moment you've been waiting for for hours, but the masses never see it that way. But because I saw it that way, I wanted something else to do with my time while I watched the game to show loving support for my mother. Spending my childhood going to museums and observatories. Her love of the game was worth it

Football, I would have acquainted myself with it out of love as well and I still to this day equate it like the gladiators fighting the lions. That's why the colosseums are shaped that way. That's why arenas are shaped that way like the old Roman colosseums wherein all happens our entertainment for the masses. I dated a model in Rome. I don't date a lot Im very picky of how I spend my time. Cone-shaped going up into the sky buildings without a roof so you can fit more people. Average joes Watch something down below that they can hardly see because they can feel the energetics of a person fighting a lion and you don't know who's going to win the person or the lion. And Kings watching from boxes.

Now sideline note: Crazy hipsters who don't like to use logic. Or gossips they think just because they have an opinion that makes it so. So, they might say a human can't beat a lion... If you don't read a book... Before Google existed humans read books to figure out what happened in the world and then they used the scientific method to figure out what could be true and what cannot be true, not just it popped into your head so it must be true. So, all hipsters right now thinking a human can't kill a lion.

This is not Facebook. Your opinion does not determine logic and humans killed lions for decades, with weapons and their bare hands in the arena in Rome which still stands.

Rome: I've been there more than a couple of times to see the statues I learned about studying mythology since I was very little. Seeing the statues in Rome I love so much it's one of my favorite things in the world. And modern-day arenas are called Coliseums for that reason. Yes, hipsters, but little history for you. Don't be a Dick. It's not a virtue. Back to the main program. So, football is built upon that, the Gladiator. It's just that there's not screaming for the bloodshed anymore. Now we scream for the points and the injury, but we still dress like the old warriors. We still paint our faces. We still yell and scream. Energy. Less warring on the streets. There's still food and feast as we watch the brutality, it's still the same subconscious programming for humans. That's what it is. That's what football is when you watch it.

Now everybody knows that I don't like playing sports anyway. It's not the way I'm built. So, the sports I play are all extreme sports. I'm a scuba diver. I ride motorcycles. I ride horses, things that involve Meditation or Extreme Earth Energy, like the God of War. In Monaco I love sitting and watching the Yachts. There are a few other things including catamaraning and parasailing, and farmers markets wherever I am in the world. My favorite Framers Market in Italy on Venice. So, I do things that I could die! every time I do it, but I don't do it for the adrenaline rush, and I don't do it ever to risk my life because I like my life. I love living. I enjoy having a life even when I don't like necessarily what's presently happening in my life.

The Madhatter's Tea Parties - We all Like Sweets Imagine Seeing It As An Energy

So, as a doctor, I try to help my clients understand the difference between that. That? Just because we're not enjoying what's happening in life doesn't mean we shouldn't appreciate living.

If You Love Pandora Hearts

Life is on this planet is a Gift

What's currently happening in your life may suck balls. Somebody might have hurt you on purpose, might've cast some spells; somebody might've sent some negative energy. Sent H force. There could be someone meditating to change your timeline, hexes, curses, family curses, intrusion to your physical space, jealous humans, hateful humans, all these isms, silliness, and not to mention hipsters JUST kidding, Nah your cruelty on the internet is e-vil. Bullies Suck.

But handle it like you are Alice In Borderland

Life You Know I Love You But

Sometimes you suck balls

(That's why people do negative energy by choice or subconscious they want to come bringing their funky vibe into your world, many people want you to think life is a terrible thing) Your thoughts create our realities. Like we are each a planet. So they want your thought to be about crap to make you use your thoughts to create crap in your world.

Think of it as if it was why are they always trying to get in your way. And selling their soul to try to make you sell yours. Trying to make it terrible.

But You go to the gumball machine and you go, "you know what, this gumball is not working for me. I'm soul, I'm eternal. I'm infinite" (and then in our last chapters, I'll teach you what to do about that negative energy being sent your way.)

But choose a new gumball and be like I'm not going to even look at this situation in this way and the me that is I'll destroy you right now and I want a new me right now.

I Love Everyday because I Love Comic Books

Do you see? Then you pull yourself up out of that situation by just going to the next multi-verse, by saying my perception creates my world. Now, a whole bunch of dick heads too because they're really, really, really mad. Matter of fact, I'm going to go here.

My mom, my grandma, every woman in my family will be shocked, but I'm going to say the word pissed because there are dick heads pissed that you are happy. There are dick heads pissed that you handle the trauma they add to your life to steal your joy because they don't like their lives. Well, guess what don't give in. Don't be sad. Don't be fearful.

A bunch of dick heads wanting to make themselves feel better by taking the smile off your face.

I've actually heard people say stuff like you're too sparkly or we're going to wipe that smile off your face, or you should know your place or we can do whatever we want to you. Or I see a new boyfriend in your space. I don't want you to be happy. I don't want you to be loved. I don't want you to be rich. I don't want you to be sexy. I don't want you to be skinny. I don't want you to be fabulous. Whatever they're saying has nothing to do with their life. It always has to do with your life. So, screw them and screw that and be happy anyway. !! I will tell you one little trick right now. It's called tsunami.

Tsunami 9 gifts of the Spirit

I teach it to the little kids. When they're stirring up all that stuff, you decide which gumball you're going to be. Nine gifts of the Spirit for those not raised in church, I use the scientific names for the tested gifts. If you pull a new gumball and you don't like that one, destroy it right then and take another one, and then you take that energy they sent, and you tsunami. That saves little kids' lives. That saves little kids' lives from school bullies, but it saves you from any energetic bully or physical bully. Tsunami is an amazing tool. I've seen it. I've even seen police that have a police brutality mentality. There was a highway patrolman... I was driving and I used to live like in the Redwoods. So, you pretty much leave the freeway, drive into the Redwood forest then you keep driving, and then you have to know which break in the trees is your turn for your driveway.

Science Is Life

So, people don't know that we have houses and sometimes you might see a little bit of yard or something. So, I was driving home and there was a highway patrolman. It was almost funny at the level of his racism. So, there was a that he was clocking, and you know how they stand there with the radar. So, he has got the radar, he's clocking it and clocking it and then he realizes that car is going over a hundred and it's about to get to him.

So, he hops in his car to go and he's like in his car ready so that when that speeder goes, he can follow the speeder because if he's ahead of him, he can't stop him and ticket him. So, he has to wait, and then he looks, and he sees a black woman in a car. She's in a little fancy SUV and the black woman's driving less than the speed limit do, do, do-ing. I always call it the meditation girls. We're always, usually pretty chill. The yoga girls are normally passive-aggressive and mean as the dick heads, literally, a snake demon is inside them. But the meditation girls connecting to source usually pretty chill. So, this woman anyways has just got a smile on her face. There's no one in her car. There's no rap coming out. As a matter of fact, there was probably, I think it was some sounds of the rain or the ocean that was playing in her car and she was just driving.

The officer now is in his car waiting for the speeder coming towards him from the left-hand side so he can get behind him.

His car is pointed so that he can get directly behind the speeding car when it comes from the left and when it passes him, as soon as it enters, he's going to go and drive right to follow the speeding car coming from the left. So, while he's sitting there, he sees this black woman in her car doing absolutely nothing but driving and just at the speed limit and peaceful, no cell phone or texting. Inside doing nothing in a gorgeous SUV with current tags. There's no reason to target this person. His subconscious is so racist that the woman coming from the right that he's looking at while he's waiting for the person doing over 100 miles an hour, down a 50 mile, an hour, or 45-mile road, depending on what part of the curves you're on, never higher than 50 miles an hour.

In some parts, the curves are so dangerous because you can't see the other car. It's 35 miles. This person's doing almost 120 because that's what the officer's radar gun said that it was clocked at. This guy is so racist he starts turning his car left to follow the black woman in the car that's doing nothing, turn his car and he's doing this back and forth. It's all happening very quickly because remember, he's got a racing car coming towards him and it's only about a mile and a half or two miles away. So, it was like 5 or 6 miles. It was a far distance when the radar picked it up. By the time he got in his car, it had between four and five miles before it would get to him. So, he knew he had time to get in his car, but he had to hurry then he sees the black woman.

So, now it is like watching some kind of crazy comedy skit because you can hear his tires and look on his face and what he's doing is going left (screech) then saying, oh, I should catch the black person because they're black. Then he backs up and he goes to the right. I better get the speeder and so his car is going left-right, left-right-left-right, left-right. cruelty based on class restrictions, be out of the race and just harm somebody who's doing nothing. Go to the right and get the real criminal. He's confused because the racism is confusing him of what is the crime. Is he going to commit a crime and go after the citizen who's doing nothing or is he going to stop a crime and most likely an accident that could kill people by going to the right and following the speeding car coming from his left?

He continued to do that to the point where you could tell his brain was in a loop. That means his racial hatred is so deep that it controls not just his mind, but his physical body's ability to function. Okay. The black woman in the car drove.

She was now out of his view. He was still doing the right-left, right-left, right-left, right-left then the speeding car comes and it's like, the hatred had an energetic vibration or wire like we all have. It could be a wire, the size of fishing line and a hook. It could be the size of a piece of thread. It could be strong as dental floss. It could be made of light. It could look like a ship's anchor. It could be thick as a tree, but the energetic racial hatred that was drawing him to go mess with the innocent citizen if he went to the left and followed the car coming from his right, who was just a black woman driving home most likely, or to a beach or to a park or to a store. It's not his business where she was going or what she was doing because she wasn't doing anything wrong.

The speeding car, he had no energetic attachment to, which is why the other subconscious of the racial hatred was able to pull him to want to chase the woman. The car came and it was like the wind from the speeding car cut the energetic cord of the racism for one woman and he went after the speeding car after looking like some weird cartoon video game of a highway patrol car going right-left, right-left.

You could hear the dirt because it would speed and he wasn't going more than a few feet, but when you're turning right, if you're straight, and matter of fact, he was angled towards his right so that when the car speeding at 120 came from his left, he could follow them quickly. He was aimed to go after the real criminal, but the energetic cord created by the hatred that exists in his body, in his cells, in his subconscious, in his mind so deeply made him keep turning that car to the left and you could hear it on the dirt and then he'd remember the speeding car and then he turned to the right. So, that little dirt literally made a V, a groove of a V deep in the dirt, right-left, right-left, right-left. He went on and so I went on because I knew that day maybe a crime would be stopped but racism doesn't only work in police stopping and shooting black people. It also works is who was driving the car at 120 miles.

Was it another officer? They're going to let him go. Was it a poor white man? They're going to give him a ticket. Was it a rich white man? They're going to let them go. Was it a cute woman? Maybe he will sexually assault her or sexually harassed her, or try to extort sex in order to get out of a ticket. These are all real crimes but when we're only worried about the ism that affects us, we forget all the running cords. See that's and on. That's why we should try to make a difference. So, sometimes my kids will be gang members and the police would arrest them for being black or Mexican or Asian or poor white or Taiwanese or Tongan or Korean. Just as gang members, they would do that, or they just dress like they were gang members because they were kids and wanting to look cool. But either way, the police would arrest them for doing nothing.

They had nothing on them. Police who were corrupt not the Good Police, Take them into the Hills or on a back street, beat the crap out of them then the police from their own pockets or from their police cars grab drugs that they confiscated other places, from robbing drug dealers. Yes, the police rob drug dealers, and then especially right below the level of drug trafficking they rob them because once the drug traffickers bring it in from ships and things like that, it gets dispersed to the Hills who can then drive down and disperse it to the neighborhoods where it's sold and where you would drive down the street and know that drugs are sold here. That kind of thing.

So, the police would have these drugs in their car and in their pockets, beat up teenagers, kids, children, people's babies is what I like to call them. Then after beating them for no reason, other than they were poor, police throw the drugs on top of them and then arrest them for drug possession which makes another demonic cycle. Another place where now they're innocent and they're in there with people who are just full of demons and they're getting sexually abused and mentally abused. Why? Because they were Chinese and poor and were in a gang. One thing I love is that I once met a guy, so cutie patootie, just so handsome, gorgeous with the most beautiful tattoos on his arms. So, I asked him, you know, this was a grown man who was a police officer, but I didn't want to start with that because I knew something was up. As a profiler, as a doctor, I knew something was up when I met him. What would my little darling wild, narcissistic hipster say? Presenting.

So, he was presenting as a police officer, but energetically, psychically he didn't feel like a police officer. As a profiler, I could assess in his stance, his wild, sexy buff-ness and his wolfy alpha male magnetic appeal, energetically that there was something more to this police officer than police work. He had been a teenage gang member hence the tattoos. He had grown up extremely poor hence the sexy appeal. Now I'm not saying poor is sexy, although some crazy hood-rat Sheneneh is likely to try to turn that into like a new way to be. What I'm saying is he turned his life around so that he could stop criminals. He's like, I got a new gang. He has a new gang, they just wear blue, and they have guns and the DA's office supports them. The law is behind them.

So, he didn't do that as a grownup. He changed and I'm not saying, oh, as soul he evolved, and he meditated. No. One day he figured out all that illegal stuff the police were doing to him and his friends or other rival gangs. He was just like; do you know what? I can stop criminals and if I enjoy fighting, I'm going to have to fight criminals and stop them. So, I'm going to become an officer and keep my neighborhoods safe this way. So, that's what he did, and even though he didn't have to. He could have taken an assignment in another neighborhood or a whole different cities police department, he liked to be what is called a beat cop meaning he doesn't drive around in his patrol car or a K-9 unit where the police officer's partner is a trained to kill German shepherd. He didn't do that. He likes to walk neighborhood in his, or similar to how he grew up wearing a police uniform, not being corrupt, and protecting his neighborhood from criminals.

Now in the neighborhood, he grew up in the shopkeepers are criminals, but they rob, robbed and are always robbing the city and some citizens based on race. They don't even take the time to break the law. They robbed the state and they're extremely, extremely racist of other people that look visually racially different than they are. But he didn't buy into that either because his soul is on its road. Got it. His soul was meant to be a good police officer because when he looked at the gumball machine, he realized he didn't like parts of who he was and what he had to do to survive. But he didn't say, you know what, I'm going to go work in a corporate office somewhere, or I'm going to start a company, or I'm going to work in construction. There are a bazillion jobs. There are so many different types of careers. You are lucky if your soul is able to figure out at a young age what helps it serve its purpose because ...soul doesn't belong to you. You belong to soul.

soul doesn't belong to you. You belong to soul. (The Caterpillar Didn't know who he was busy asking Alice)

That's what our new chapter is about. You belong to soul. Now, luckily for me, I like Kawaii. Those of you who don't know what

Kawaii is, I don't mean the Island (Kauai) in Hawaii. I mean, K-A-W-A-I-I. It's a look where everything's fun. Toast has eyeballs and smiles and so does ice cream, so do suitcases. I even do Kawaii art and we have fabric lines and classes because I believe. I don't just like Kawaii because it looks silly because my first thing is I love corsets. I love glitter. I love costumes. I love jewels. Not just gold, more like aurora borealis stones. I like pearls. I like natural crystals and gemstones, antique jewelry and Faberge eggs. I like things that are beautiful. because I think beautiful, elegant things add a higher vibration into the world, add more light into someone's day. But Kawaii adds joy even if you're just evil, so evil, you can make the whites of your eyes turn black at will. You have no light left. You may not even be the soul born in that body. You're the thing that took over that body and you are dark to the core. Who can resist a boiled egg with a smile and long lashes? So, I love Kawaii. So, we're going to talk about some resources, some things that can give us joy when the world is trying to give us crap.

So, what my parents did, each of them together and separately, my parents took me to experience beautiful things in the world. Didn't teach me about any ugly things so I was only able to understand the ugly things as a science. Even problems within my own family where they would use euphemisms. I didn't know what to call those things until I was a grownup and in university and applied science to it. But I grew up with holistic health, not a lot of metaphysics because I grew up in a family where you are Baptist or Catholic and all the women or most of the women are born with what's called prophetic dreams, where God gives you messages of the present, answers, how to fix problems and visions of the future so you know, what's coming or visions of the past so you can resolve it. Then I was born with clairvoyance.

Alice SOS I was born with clairvoyance

I was born with a lot of gifts, but clairvoyance means you can see clearly In the world and in Dreams. You can see energy, you can see the world, you can see other worlds. Changing Life in Fundamental Ways DOWN THE RABBIT HOLE

You can see maybe looking at some woman and she seems like she's really pretty, but she's really evil. So when we look you see the monster she really is. So, when you look at her, you'll see a beautiful woman and what she wants you to see. When I look at her, I will see an evil creature from a fairy tale. So, she might look like a wolf or she might look like an alligator, or she might look like she has horns. I mean, like in a Snow White kind of horned woman, not like a stereotypical picture of a devil horn. Because I don't believe necessarily that it looks like that in the spiritual world or the physical world or the real world that kind of thing. I think evil operates more in racism and unkindness and sexism and rape of men and children. I worked a lot of years to stop the rape of children. So, I wasn't just saying, please don't rape children. I was healing the victims, but I was doing documentaries, TV shows.

I mean, I had a radio show, but on my radio show, it was mostly like life coaching, self-help spirituality, and education for all Souls and exposure of choosing not to educate trying not to provide a future for the poor. But my TV show was about staying happy. So, I've had two television shows. One was a TV news show, and one was a DIY show where it shows you how to apply the use of creativity and art to build your happiness so that when you walk into the world and somebody else's soul may be being tricked or may have volunteered or born into things that are just purely, purely low vibrational. When I say low vibrational, that's a nonjudgmental way to say dark, mean, evil. I know I see it differently what I've taught some people and they view it like this, things that uplift, things that push down or pollute. So, one of my teachers taught me early on that if it doesn't uplift, it's not God meaning sometimes, you know, when you were having a hard time or even if you're having a great time and you get targeted by somebody else's energetic thought like telepathy.

I also HAVE Telepathy

Alice In The Country Of Hearts and Gifts to remember everyone is Soul

So, those of us who have telepathy will HEAR not like clairaudience. We don't hear what something is trying to tell us. We hear the stuff people will wish we couldn't find out their secret or things they themselves do not know (consciously). We always know as soul when we remember we belong to GOD. We hear God tell us the thought of a being or a soul or of a situation or an object or an animal which is different because a clairaudient would hear if they went somewhere and they're helping an investigative team or they're looking for a lost child. They might hear the things that the child said during their death or during the assault or during the kidnapping or they might hear like in a remote viewing way. They might hear a conversation that the kidnapper is having with the child whereas the clairvoyants will see the child and the kidnapper sitting in the car having this conversation. But they may only see a street sign that they pass that kind of tells them where the car was.

So, where the kid might be alive or dead. But a clairaudient is going to hear the conversation that they're saying. What is said like in a visual movie with sound. The telepath will hear the thoughts the child is having during that time plus the things the child wants to say, even telling you whether or not they're alive or dead. The telepath will also hear the thoughts of the killer. Are they evil? Are they a demon? Are they human with a childhood that they're telling you as an excuse for what they are doing or you're seeing their demented brain? The reason it's called dementia because in the 1800s we believed as a species that all mental illness was a spiritual intrusion/pollution. It was either a spiritual attack, or it was a spiritual infestation, a spiritual embodiment of some other soul's entity or other soul's energy inside of your body. That would cause mental illness. That's what was believed in the 1800s and there are a lot of Catholic exorcists who believed and believe that that's what all mental illness is now. So, if we take it down a notch in the spiritual world and bring it to the physical world for better understanding.

When I say better understanding, I mean, people (scratching their head) going that can't happen. While others or (scratching their head) going that happens to me.

(Another joke for hipsters) skip to the next paragraph if you like if you are not a hipster (hipsters asked me 8 years ago to be their life coach/therapist). Remember hipsters, this is not Facebook. There's no comment section so listen so you can learn about the world and be happy. Stop committing suicide, be more kind so you know what your unkindness is doing. So, when we understand it in this way, now we can say that Victorian belief and the exorcists' belief that mental illness, (depression is also a mental illness) inside is someone else's energy. Now we get the real world. Let's do this. Let's do this. Listen, listen, listen. Linda... It is when you say bullying things when you make those rude comments. Hipsters, why do you think I'm always on your case about just saying anything in a comment because that's energy.

Words are energy and you're putting your or funky energy inside you, like a wild, crazy demon into somebody else's body that has been registering in them, staying in their space, and presenting itself as mental illness. Sadness or Hopelessness. So, you are the demon that crawled in somebody and gave them a mental illness with your unkind words, thoughts, actions, and deeds, just like the gladiator games that we talked about a few chapters ago.

Remember the crowd watches while a human fights a lion and they're there to cheer on the excitement of the bloodshed. That's demonic behavior. People died so other people could watch it for sport. You trolling and attacking people verbally is an energetic attack. You're being used by evil to cause people to want to commit suicide. You never realized it, we just now for the first time in human history have a generation wherein people say they want to commit suicide and their friends' girlfriends write back in texts and on comments on social media ,yeah do it. Or comment "Everybody hates you anyway". "The world would be a better place". "Your family will be better off". You never stepped back or listened to yourself or re-read your comments on social media to realize something evil is wearing you. Something evil is using you. Your meat costume is being used to make other people want to die and you think it's funny. Forgive let's clean that, as an Empath we know energy floats into the air. Floats in the air like when in a comic book and you need to draw those lines in the air for the reader to see something stinks in the air.

So, for the first time in human history, we have had to pass laws that say, if you do that, you're committing murder if the person dies or attempted murder, if they attempt suicide and fail. I have met hipsters coming to me for life coaching, which we call Happiness coaching because you know, my personality is I get your Happiness back, get your joy back. Do you see?

Shake your butt like a rubber duck. You know those non-stick pans. You better turn yourself into a freaking non-stick rubber ducky because people have done it. I've been shaking my butt on stage doing talks for 18 years. Shaking my ducky butt to get my audiences to do it with me. We now know people make rubber duckies look like nurses, police officers, pirates, gangsters. They're making rubber duckies look like stuff, but no matter what, rubber ducky face, you see a rubber duck, every subconscious of humans on the planet, even ones who've never seen a rubber duck before. When you see a rubber ducky, that's some joy. That's some joy and so many, many, many years ago, many years ago, long before they started painting rubber duckies to look like other stuff there was a yellow duck, and they walk with their little waddle and it causes every human, I don't care how evil you are, how gangster you are. Do you know how many gangsters there are with really good hearts that just grew up feeling so unsafe they wanted to be the bigger threat or had to be in order not to starve or be a victim or to protect their mother?

Rubber Duckies Are A Spiritual Weapon YEP

So, they smile, and rubber duckies are one of the things that can make anybody smile. So, your purpose of you being a rubber ducky sometimes, especially the non-stick rubber ducky is not to make the person looking smile. That might be a byproduct, but it is a Spiritual Weapon. Yeah. Rubber ducky, a spiritual weapon. You turn yourself into the non-stick rubber ducky and you shake your ducky butt. Now everybody knows, even though I love stuff, being fun and I love corsets and I love costumes and I love ballgowns and I love dressing like I'm in a 1930s and 40s detective movie, with gangsters and molls and I got ta wear a straight skirt and a suit. One of my ex-boyfriends he's so cute. You know I only have eight ex-boyfriends but one of them, he used to call 1940s suits my uniform because even though I had so many suits, tons of suits, tons of dresses, tons of skirts, all my skirts were straight skirts and all my suits had straight skirts. So, he boiled it down to you're always in stilettos, a straight skirt, like a 1940s pencil skirt. Not just a straight skirt because some of those are like dowdy librarians. I'm more like a sexy librarian. So, it's like, she would be like a super sexy librarian.

Well, guess what? I am not really goofy. I'm quite serious. I'm quirky. I'm funny but I don't like looking or feeling stupid. People that are goofy don't care if they look or feel stupid. They have fun physically using their body to do things to make people laugh. I'm witty. I will say stuff to make people laugh and I will clown like the Dickens. So, when I say clown, I mean like a clown, somebody for acting a fool. So, if somebody is doing something like really, really evil. I taught teenagers forever and I was 21. I was literally 21 years old when I started teaching, I was 22 because a month later, I'm an October baby but it took the end of the school year. So, school starts in August. I was 21 years old. I had students that I was only four years older than, four to five years older than my students, depending on when their birthdays happen. Then a couple of months into that, my birthday came, and I turned 22. But when you first turn a new age, you're not really that age yet because you don't know what that age is. So, you really are still your previous age, about three to six, sometimes seven months into your new age before you master being that.

So, the school year ended before. I really like felt like how you feel when you're 22, as opposed to how you feel when you're 21. So, just imagine those teenagers. Teenagers say anything they want to you. As a matter of fact, when you're very beautiful teenagers flirt with their teachers, teenagers call their teacher everything under the book, every curse word, every name because you're making them do work. They lie on you. They manipulate other grownups. Teenagers do some really evil stuff all to not do their work, all to not have homework. All because you made them do an assignment. All because they didn't do their work. And then you gave them a grade based on points and they didn't have enough points because they didn't do their work. But then they'll lie and call you names. So, you can't like, just forget when you were a teenager. WE we all teenagers once. So, I always crack jokes and say stuff back to them with the exception of racial slurs - that gets you detention, not jokes.

Alice Academy No hate in our classroom of any kind BECAUSE IT doesn't belong in our world.

If you say racial slurs in my classroom, I'm not going to think of something witty to say back to you. I'm going to think of something very stern and adult-like to say back to you because I don't want hate in my classroom. Not hate of homophobia, not hate of sexism. Boys don't get to talk under girls' clothes. That's a very old saying for sexual harassment. Boys don't get to talk under girls' clothes. Girls don't get to be mean to boys they think are nerdy or ugly. Nobody gets to tease my gay or transgender kids before a transgender, even had a name. No hate in our classroom of any kind. So, then I am very adult about that. But if you just say something mean like, you can call me the B-word, I will come back with a joke. So, I will be like dangerous I was taught to read by drag Queens. Do you see? So, it's like, do not mess with me and I don't mean the way I read Shakespeare and Freud and Nietzsche and Agatha Christie and Dante and Bronte and Keats or the other thousands of classical literature that I have read. I mean, in the way you look at a human figure out something about them that's not quite right that they may not like. That is hilariously funny that won't crush their ego, but will make them think in a halt. So, a good drag queen read is a read where you don't know you've been read until you think about it because it makes you laugh at yourself, but it also makes you look at yourself. It makes you look at your action and make it look at what you did. School is supposed to be making citizens. Building functional members of society.

So, kids have found ways to be very cruel to each other, to the point where it results in suicide, and then we have a lot of teenagers now they'd be like, I'm a witch. I'm going to cast a spell so you can all tell my demons to make your chair break. Literally, kids saying that sitting in a chair in a classroom, this happened in a classroom. A child stared at me, stared at me, stared at me, and said with her mouth, I'm telling my demons to attack you and break your chair and then just sit there instead of doing her work saying break, break, break. I have been a therapist for a lot of witches, and I was taught in women's studies class in university, witches are a part of women's history and by my mom who was a feminist, who raised me around a whole bunch of feminists. One thing you know, when you're around and I hate to say, actual feminist, cause now there are like 6, really there are 19 ways to be a feminist, but there are 6 or 7 that you usually see. So, feminism is not supposed to be another hate crime.

So, you're not supposed to be a feminist because you hate men. You're not supposed to be a feminist because you fear, men. You're supposed to be a feminist because you value women. Women's history and yourself as a woman. Well, guess what? Most people calling them feminists. Now they don't get that. So, they abuse other women. They attack women out of envy. They berate men. I mean, it's crazy. But if all of that's happening in a classroom and there's only one grownup, the grownups aren't doing anything. Most of them aren't even qualified teachers. You do realize that if you check your childrens' teacher's teaching credential, check out your kid's teacher and look up their teaching credential. You're going to find that for the past 18 years. Okay. Imagine how many years we you go to middle school and high school. Those are three years span and four years span so how many generations over the last 18 years have had unqualified people in the classroom. People who never went to school to be a teacher, people who aren't university trained to be a teacher, people who never took child psychology, never studied Pavlov, didn't have a degree or a drive in life.

There is more than data that makes a teacher. They had cruelty based on class restrictions and their racism said because your kids are a different race than them and/or poor that that unconscious unqualified uneducated teacher must know more than your kids so classism that makes them a teacher. This was very profitable for school districts because actual teachers cost actual money. The federal government spends about $182,000 a year per kid for your kid's education, especially in the poorest neighborhoods. So, schools are really overfunded. But what they do instead of hiring a teacher, that's paid by scale in two directions the number of college units they have and the number of years they've been teaching, that's how the pay scale works. The more units, the more money, the more years, the more money required by union contract. So, if you hire someone who didn't train to be a teacher, they only have the units of a bachelor's degree, not the additional units it takes to get a teaching credential or any advanced training as a teacher or all the units that come with the LEGALLY Required additional teaching credentials.

So, they break the law because it's against federal and state law. It's an embezzlement of federal funds because the federal funds are provided so that citizens have an education, which means school districts have what is called a 'fiduciary responsibility to educate'. But because of racism and remember this is the nice way to talk about it.

So, we understand the small nuances, kind of like when you're black and you walk into your neighborhood where you live and your neighbors think you're visiting because the racism in their head is so deep they know for sure they don't have any black neighbors. So, they call the police because you're in their neighborhood. First of all, in America, anybody can be in anyone's neighborhood period. There's no law that says you can't go to a certain neighborhood. But there is violence to keep you out. There's cruelty based on class restrictions that says you can't go to a certain neighborhood because of the violence which is another illegality by citizens of that neighborhood. But other than a military base, in this country you're American, you can go there. It just some people made it deadly for you to do so or uncomfortable calling you names or threats of violence but remember everything's energy. So now imagine you're in a school system and you want the poor kids to stay poor and if they have what we had when we were little kids, women because elementary school usually there's one male teacher because elementary kids usually are kind of fragile in their emotions.

So, a lot of men teach high school and middle school, but traditional gender roles made it so a lot of women for the nurturing of the little ones. Well, these women came from the South. They were not there for the nurturing of the little ones. They loved us, but they literally came from the Southern States to California to teach in poor neighborhoods to make sure the kids got a good education so they could have a good future. Well, guess what? The whole racist world didn't like that. See there is a racist world the, world is not racist and race is not based on the race of the person there's a sector of our world who are programmed to be racist, I'm trying to be clear that way down on a subconscious level without their permission far before they're grown-ups. Not everybody in the world, but the racist world didn't like that because now you have poor kids becoming rich grownups. ALL RACISM is to control CLASS. To control ability to make money. So, to fix that in our nice way to talk about cruelty based on class restrictions, they made sure that your kids did not have teachers, real teachers, teachers didn't have teachers. They had people, they called teachers illegally, but they didn't have people with credentials or university training. They had emergency credentials, which means you should only teach for 30 days. Not even, hopefully not 30 straight days. It's 30 days in a school year because they figure you can't do too much damage because the school year is 183 to 188 days, depending on the state you're in required by the federal government because the government is paying for learning minutes.

Because remember our federal government is paying for butts in seat per hour and they measure it by educational minutes. That's why you can differ in the number of days because the federal requirements for education are based on minutes, minutes of learning time. You can't count recess. You can't count lunch. So, what do you think about the embezzlement of these school districts that the kids are being given A's and B's, so the parents don't complain and the school day, which is a six-hour day of learning time, four and a half for ones that have the little split schedule? As long as you end up with the federally mandated minutes per year, you can have as many holidays or as few holidays as you want. That's why school schedules look different because it's based on federal learning minutes that they are being more than paid well for. The money is usually misappropriated but the kids are allowed to play video games and watch movies and these people with no teaching credentials, no university training, were allowing the kids to watch movies.

The kids weren't telling because you would like to play games and watch movies all day at work too, and still get an A or a B to the point where when the state caught them and fined them and they got in trouble for it, the solution wasn't to hire teachers with credentials because that would have messed up the calling classism/racism. What they did was the districts lied and said, the district gave the teachers the credential, which they did not get any training and they didn't give them any training and they replaced the computer so the computers didn't have a DVD drive so that they couldn't play the movies. So, all the uncredentialed racists posing as teachers did making sure that the poor didn't have an education while collecting a teacher's salary and the benefits of home loans at 2% interest, because you taught at a poor school. The benefit of erasing all your college loans, because you taught at a poor school when you weren't teaching anything. They brought their computers from home and signed up a personal Netflix account so they can still let the kids watch movies or let them play games on their phone, text, do anything but learn and work.

When you're a teenager and you're a little kid, cause this starts by second grade doing this with these uncredentialed teachers. The reason most grownups have a second-grade level education is that most people that teach kindergarten and first grade started teaching before this and anybody teaching kindergarten and first grade that's good teachers meant to be there They don't retire until they have a white Mrs. Claus bun. So, that person teaches for 30 or 40 years. So, imagine you learn at that grade level and then you don't learn again.

When you're little, you're just like, "yay, we get to watch a moviez". Yay, we get to do what we want. But when you're a grownup, you don't say yay when you can't figure out basic stuff but that's what happens. That's how we have so many grownups without an education. It was purposeful miseducation based on racism fake name for classism. So I opened a store to fix this. If I say right now, big, giant crowd, what would I say? If I say it's not racism, you're supposed to yell back. It's classism.

All cruelty based on class restrictions is money even if you are in your head, the race that's in power, and get to do racism to other people. It's a trick. It's a trick so you won't want to be wealthy because you already have a superpower issue. It's your racial hate. You have the power to harm other people. Demons. Oh, don't you have a superpower, but do you have the superpower to have lobster every day? Yeah. Lobster is yummy, you see pizzas yummy and the way my personality is, I wouldn't say I prefer pizza over lobster, but what about some lobster pizza? Got it. You don't have those options. They made you work hard. Do the dirt jobs. Meaning in the dirt, you go home dirty. Whether you are covered in dirt, oil, sewage, poop, garbage, whatever you are covered in, but you have this superpower of racially hating other people and historically not getting in trouble for it.

PEACE

When I say historically, you should see the shocked look as a profiler. What I am amazed by is now the shock on people's faces who are being arrested for shooting and killing other humans.

If you look at their picture, there's no anger. They're shocked like, oh my goodness, how'd I get in trouble for that because on a subconscious level, as a society, we told millions and billions of people do what you will, like Lord Crowley said. I don't know how many people know about Aleister Crowley, but I know there are millions of people who practice and follow what he did and what he believed. So, there's a phrase called "do what thy will" meaning spiritually don't follow any other universal laws. Don't follow any other spiritual laws that will keep light in your body. Do whatever you want spiritually. This does make you complete darkness but do what you will. That's what racism is, do what you will. That's your team as you're Christian and racist, you're Catholic and racist, you're Presbyterian and racist, you're Baptist and racist. Even if you're racist to racists.

Something evil gets to use you. It gets to live inside you unlike one of my friends, who's a very famous witch, a very old witch likes the work that I do to help victims recover from multi-millionaire pedophiles. Or the multimillionaires that I help being their life coach and Happiness joy coach and helping them get out of relationships where they literally married crazy evil married female demons. With my work now They get free from that and so I have friends of every type because I don't judge. So, this particular friend is a witch, even though I got tons of friends that are multimillionaires, who are now happy and no longer married to demons or girls presenting themselves as subservient or docile or young or innocent when really they came to harm them and steal their money and never loved them and say that to them.

Cheshire Cat and Tea Parties

Things that hate makes us do. A couple who have lost their money and their wife left them the next day, after a long Batman villain speech about how she never loved him in the first place. That's why we do our Did you Buy a Mannequin class? That's why we do that class.

But my friend, who's like an old, old, super famous witch said that which you witches, witches you. What that means is all that evil and negativity you are pulling in and all that, the evil they got put up on you so somebody would trick you to not understand racism is classism. So, teaching you to be racist is the upper-class teaching you to stay poor and out of their way and go fight their war and attack the rest of the poor and call it racism. So you won't be there to interrupt our night at the opera.

So, you never have their life, but you do have the right to be full of hate. So, that which you're witching is witching you. So, you're full of hate. You're full of anger. So that results in extra anger, extra hate, childhood abuse, the abuse of your children, spousal abuse, bar room brawls, this anger that wells up in you. I've seen people so racist that their racism is nothing but anger and evil and it makes them tremble.

So, just if they see a Chinese person, just if they see a black person, if they see a Mexican person and they see a Taiwanese, they see a Tongan. Even in Hawaii, they'll be in Hawaii hating Hawaiians. If you look real close, you don't have to study hard, but watch the corpuscles swell, meaning through their skin you can see red coming to the surface, little red veins. Not the big veins. You see little, tiny ones then some of them just turn all the way beet red. Got it. That's evil showing itself. That's anger and hate inside them just cause you to breathe. Now have compassion for the being who got tricked into not even knowing that they are Soul and have a family working hard building America. Those jobs build our country. Those dirty jobs. Keep our country running, build our country, being tricked into hating so evil can use their bodies and so the rich can use their physical bodies. while keeping you in poverty because it's about racism is keeping the poor in check.

Racism is not just the haves and have-nots, it's the have everything or have nothing but seem to have everything because you are surrounded by stuff to feel like you have something. That's why you're taught to overbuy.

The poor are programmed to overbuy. That's classism hiding as racism. The poor are programmed to spend and consume and be surrounded by stuff and they make sure you can afford it no matter how little money you have, but make sure you spend every cent you have. That's cruelty based on class restrictions. All evil manipulations is about money and class and spiritual war. Therefore The spiritual war that says the dark doesn't have a body. Now there are people whose family has done darkness or dark magic for generations who have literally dedicate your body when you're born to darkness. So, never think that dark is not just walking in a human body, and it had to invade everywhere.

But all isms including cruelty based on class restrictions is to make sure dark is stronger in you than light so that you can even uncreate your own goals. Now, as someone who practices black magic or someone who's spiritually dark, they always want a wife or a girlfriend who is light because that also represents creativity. The flow right of fortune, not the theft of fortune, but the flow of fortune. That's what light does; light draws. That's why Cinderella hums even though she's dirty and cleaning because she still has her Happiness, light, joy.

She still has her light. She has her gratitude which is another spiritual tool, and I don't mean spiritual weapon, which we'll talk about in a different chapter, but spiritual tool gratitude because it'll erase and gratitude kills hopelessness, hate, and darkness out of your space. So, when darkness doesn't have what it needs to sends demons to go gather what they want or entities or ghosts to go gather what they want. When they want to create something, they take your light or light from somewhere in the world because light creates. There is a big difference between the words manifest and actualize. Manifest means whatever it takes, whatever I have to use, whatever I'm going to let use me. I'm going to force what I want. That's why I tell people when people are like, oh, I'll pray for you. Please don't. I would rather witches pray for me, and the witches know that's no offense to witches.

Respect for women's history and all people's choices because there are male witches too. Everybody has free will. Respect your choices. Kiss. I forget that little gangster way. Shout out. It might be called shout-out. I'm not so sure, but I usually blow a kiss, put my hand to my mouth and go mwah, blow a kiss.

Got it. I do that to babies too whenever I see babies, but you want to know babies are light. Not every baby because I have met two babies who were from those families who are just straight demons, and they were too but the whites of their eyes were black because it wasn't anything in there. I called 30 people who meditate, who are metaphysical, who are Christians and I all had them pray about that baby and they all didn't know I was asking others. So, I didn't call a group of 30 people. I called 30 people who did not know each other, who all have spiritual practices that differ from each other, and asked them to check on one thing, that baby. They all came back with that's not a baby, that's a demon, not a baby. Got it.

So, another time it was the little girl of a church that says they're Christian, but they just added Jesus to their name about 100 years after they were founded to cover up what they really do, and their daughter was literally stabbing her siblings with stuff and then laughing to the point where they put locks on their doors to protect them from her getting in. But somehow she would still get through deadbolt locks without a key. We'll say it like that.

So, they wanted me to see if I could talk to her so that God could take over her body and what had taken over her body would leave it.

So, I tried, well, I shouldn't say tried. I let the little girl's conscious mind know that her subconscious was a void, literally, meaning nothing was there but darkness. There wasn't pain trapped. There wasn't family trauma. She had a great dad. She had a wonderful mom. Got it. But the spiritual practices and the ritual is done around her while it was being called Christian did it.

See when people who do magic, do rituals, they know some stuff might, what is that phrase? Some stuff might happen. Stuff might break loose that kind of thing. Things might go buck wild. They know it so they put up protocols and safeties for if something goes wrong if something comes in if something... They put protocols. for people that are saying they're Christian but doing rituals while also saying the rituals are Christian when they're dark magical because they are hate-filled. So, if you're Christian and you're a heck of a racist and you're doing a ritual, guess who's coming to dinner.

Okay. So, that's what happened and the other little girl I told her when you stab your siblings, I said, I know you think, you know what evil is but when you stab your friends, when you stab your siblings, when you hurt people and laugh, that is the devil. That's what the devil is. She just kind of looked and smiled like I know the devil very well. Then I was like, so you know you're evil.

Then another different set of parents, same religion, different daughter, different parents, different house, different state even. Her child was literally drawing demons, drawing dragging people in the hell, and drawing things where she had a ball, and she would take the ball from the person and the ball would be yellow or blue or green. She would turn and drop it into a cavern, a pit that she drew, a mountain, a canyon, and the mountains and canyons were always red, black, and orange. So, they were either black or they look like they were on fire, and she would draw herself taking someone's light and turning it dark or, or giving it to darkness. She would draw the craziest looking beings ever. This was a little girl. And then by the time she was a teenager, her mother was scared. Her mother was scared to live with her own child.

So, racism is that level of hate because that's, what's running through you, whether you sitting in a pew with a gold embossed Bible or not. So, there are nice ways to talk about this when we understand what it really is. It's not because you called somebody the N-word or the C-word or the S-word, depending on their race and words change. What's a bad word, changes culturally and geographically and it also changes by age. So, all you have to do is be a teacher and have all the kindergarteners telling somebody teacher, teacher, or somebody said the S-word. Don't overreact to kindergarteners the S-word is stupid. It's not shit, it's stupid. The S-word is not shit to a kindergartener. The S-word is stupid. Stupid is the bad word but evil doesn't work in that way. It's much more sneaky, right? You're not evil if you go to church.

Do you know how many churches I've been to where the pastor has a sex demon? Thank God that God sent me to yoga festivals and to meditation retreats where I would meet boys. When I say boys, I mean men because I come from a family where the girls stay with the girls and the boys stay with the boys and I was like Scarlet O'Hara, and I have way more friends that are men than women. So, I say the boys because I'm the girl, that kind of thing. Yeah. Guess what turns out pretty evil, yeah, because God does what sometimes doesn't make sense to you or church. So, God sent me and I teach meditation so you can connect with God. So, you're not taking deals along the way. Stuff and people saying they can give you spiritual gifts. If you let them be in your body, why don't you be a medium? And tell my cousin what? I forgot to tell her before I died. Right? You don't even know if that's really the ghost talking to you. It could be something evil pretending to be a ghost who needs you to tell their cousins something.

So, I have told 30,000 people connect with God here. God, let your gifts develop and be patient. Don't take deals unless you want to take deals. Knowingly take deals if you want to take deals, but don't be tricked into a deal. Got it. So sometimes God will send you somewhere where you don't think you should go, or church will tell you shouldn't go because church not everyone don't ask God anything. So, people at church ask that ask God, they'll be like Mia we're praying for you. We've got you don't worry. They're like, sometimes people think they wonder if you're even listening to God, but we always pray. We even call other churches, and the answer always comes back. Nope Mia is fine. Still, just God Mia's listening to, it really is God nothing's tricking her. Well, guess what? When God told me to go to the meditation festival, I was teaching meditation and I ran into the tantra boys. God said, do not talk to him. I was like, wow. And then later that guy showed up in my dream that night trying to have sex with me, but I meditate, and I connect with God, so I know when something that's not me or not God is trying to be in my space.

So, I knew that I was not having a dream as a fantasy about that guy, but that, that guy either on his subconscious level was attracted to me or on his conscious level was invading my space and having sex with my spirit. So, the tantra girls, do the same thing. Now, this tantra practice is supposed to be you're in a couple and you and the person that you're in a relationship connect sexually on an energetic level, have sex on a deeper level. You're intimate as physical bodies but you're also intimate as souls. But the hollow girls, if they want a trick, the ones casting spells and harming multimillionaires and blocking their true love and attacking their true love to the point where we got to do the spiritual stuff back. The tantra was being used as rapist. So now the tantra women have like a Me Too movement against the tantra boys.

They call that it the distant rape. Even though it's your spiritual self, spiritual self is part of yourself, just like your body is. You just don't always see it especially if you don't meditate, but your spiritual self is always there. So, I tell people *who don't meditate, or maybe they don't listen to God, or they don't have psychic gifts just think of it as your energetic body.*

So, when someone comes into your energetic body sexually, it could be just a thought they're attracted to you. My mom used to say, you can't hold people responsible for their thoughts just because you can hear them, Mia. They don't know you can hear them. So, imagine an energetic body and sexual intrusion would be they know they're sending you their energy sexually it's not just their thoughts. Got it. But the body would still have the same energy received if they just thought about it. So, a boy likes you. I know some men don't like being called boys, but I don't usually hang out with men like that because they have too much anger attached to whether or not they get called boys. It's always based on anger. Girls, same thing, women that don't like being called girls. It's attached to some kind of anger. Don't be a sexist and common girl. Call me a girl. When I'm 80, call me a girl. I'm a girl. I got to VJ, and I love being a girl and I don't have any anger towards the sexism that happens in the world because it's the same as the racism in the classes something evil trying to distract me from BEING Soul

I mean, it's all ism to trick soul and let hate run through your system. Let hate have your body and hate doesn't get to have my body. I'm a girly girl. I'm very frilly so I don't mind that at all. Call me a girl, go ahead. Most men, I know they're playboys or they used to be playboys, or they are very alpha, manly men. So, they like being called the boys because they consider themselves the boys I'm going out with the boys. That's what they say to their wives, the boys and I are leaving for the weekend. So, I don't get into those politics where it's certain men would be like for political power, never call me a boy. I'm like, I don't have time for that. There's too much hate running through your system and if I date you, it will be running through my system.

Always remember when you have sex with someone physically, you have sex spiritually. That's why they used to call it 1490 to 1870s the beast with two backs because your energetic field becomes one and the way to understand that in the physical world would be, and I haven't found a better analogy yet, but red Jell_O and green Jell_O and you know I specialize in the brain.

As a doctor, there are other color combinations and I can run you through what the other colors would do to the subconscious, and it wouldn't be as effective as these two color combinations and descriptive of what happens to you. So, you are red Jell_O or your green Jell_O and they are the other color. So, I'll make you green Jell_O because I always usually make you rich yellow whenever I tell this. So, for this example, you are green Jell_O, they're red Jell_O. When you make out the red and green Jell_O mix. When sex is over, a lot of their Jell_O goes into your Jell_O. A lot of your Jell_O goes into their Jell_O then you pull apart. Well, when you pull apart, I mean you leave for the day you go to sleep for the night, I'll see you for breakfast, honey, whether it's your husband or something like that. Gender doesn't matter in this. So, same-sex, couple, any soul having sex with another soul's physical body, this is what happens and then I'll tell you what energetically happens if you only have sex energetically by choice. Like texting. Now when it's over and you're like, okay, honey, I'll see you tonight when I get home from work or okay, boyfriend, I'll see you next time you fly into town if you have a long-distance relationship, you are not green Jell_O anymore. You don't get all the red Jell_O out of you. You get some of that and red and green mixed together makes brown and the lightest being gets the trash and the dark being gets all their trash healed and steals your light by choice, on purpose or by accident, end up with some of your goodness and your blessings and you end up with their trash and your trash.

So, when people have energetic sex, they're trying to do something with that energy.

There are some people who would like the negative energy that came off of both of you for them to hold it and use it for something else and the positive energy that comes off of the both of you and use it and save it for something else. But that's other people consciously doing that and knowing about energy. This is just every human when you have physical sex. That's what happens part of them is in your space. That's why when I help victims get those people out of you, just like when you break up with somebody, get those people out of you. When you're mad at somebody, get those people out of you, forgive, get them out of you, clean, get them out of you.

So, this is a spiritual tool. The knowledge to your conscious mind being told this in itself by itself, because I've said it, wrote it, taught it in a class, becomes a spiritual tool because now, you know, you don't need to just take a shower you need to clean yourself. Depending on who you're dealing with, you might need to get parts of yourself back, not just get rid of them. Each soul has a body and that's where your energy belongs.

So, it doesn't show more love, just like overbearing parents. If your kid is schizophrenic, if your kid picks their fingernails until they bleed somebody, usually an overbearing parent's energy is in their space or sexual abuse is in their space. Somebody else's energy is the most powerful force in their space is what they've been led to believe. But you are soul, you are infinite, you have complete ownership of that body even if you sell your soul because the soul was not yours to sell. It always belonged to somebody else. It always belonged to the creator. When you're Native American, we say the creator being, when you're Irish, you say the great spirit, the all, that kind of thing. When you're Baptist, you would say, God. If you're a go-between you say, Jesus.

When I say go-between the physical Lord that came down here, which was also God, depending on if you're Baptist or Catholic. CHRIST. So, what you do is you go to who you want to own your soul and I would say, God. So, I would say God, or I in lecture great spirit. See, I wouldn't say mother moon. I would say mother moon, thank you for cooling the earth so that we don't all burn to death because we can't handle the sun burning all the time. Thank you for shining and controlling the waters so that the water stays in the ocean and in the sea and in the river, instead of going all over the land and flooding it. Thank you, mother moon, for doing that. I would say that, right, but if something's up with a soul, I'm going to say, God, I just want you in me. I don't want somebody else energy in me, even people I love, I don't want them inside of me. I want me and God inside of me and the rest of you all evicted. The rest of you all hit the road. You don't get to stay inside of me.

gratitude which is another spiritual tool

So, when somebody casts a spell, they're really taking energy or sending a being to be in your space, to try to pollute you so they lower your vibe, or they hurt you or hurt your health or hurt your finances because that foreign negativity is invading like a little war. So, then you act like a warrior, and you declare war like that game. I don't know if children still play that game, but it was like an old game our parents used to let us play where you just take a deck of cards, like a poker card, not a tarot deck, but you take like a poker deck and you go with three cards. I declare war. Well, I guess that's four cards I declare war. I can't remember now, it's three or four cards, but whatever the cards come up, whoever had the highest card wins the war.

So, if you have too much fear, you have overbearing parents, you have anger, you have racism in your space. When that invader comes, you don't even fight the war. They've got other troops inside of you, based on the vibe you're keeping inside. Based on the fear you're keeping inside, based on the hatred you're keeping inside, based on envy, based on the anger, the unforgiveness. What you want to be is like, their troops come here, you're outnumbered, and you get stomped down, kicked out, whatever it is, however you want to visualize it. GLOW. So, the tantra boys have mastered the spiritual world because tantra men are supposed to master certain sexual levels of energy in the spiritual world so that it's like three people having sex in different places. You're having sex with your wife, your boyfriend, whatever never come for me. Do not come for me. I will tell you this now. Don't ever, ever, ever as my reader, as my audience, as my students come for me with crazy gender stuff, because my mom was a lesbian feminist, and I have fought for gender rights 37 years.

Now, obviously, she wasn't always a lesbian feminist because my parents were married, but after their divorce, probably another five or 10 years after. I could never figure out when she knew because she said, one of her boyfriend's told her she was a lesbian and then women told her she was a lesbian then she figured out and decided she must be a lesbian. But I have fought for gender rights for you to be whatever gender you decide as a part of my belief that God gave us free will.

So, I've always protected that since I was like 14 years old. I had the idea when I was 12, but I didn't know what, where I would stand up for those rights, other than not take part in it and protect little kids in school, when I was in elementary school that I thought were gay or transgender and stop bullies from hurting them. As I grew up, I just stopped other people from hurting anybody for any reason and that included gender. Then I've done some costumes, some comics, some cosplay photoshoots, some photoshoots to protect transgender rights when it comes to sex change operations and Christians weren't pleased with that and I was not pleased with Christians for gossiping, backstabbing each other and bringing the devil into people's lives.

So, we don't always like everything somebody does, but it's each soul's job to do what it is supposed to do as a soul. So, I just felt, I don't think people should be bullied by hate because it's just that they think different. The bullies are not who are shooting up the schools. School shooters when you look, it's not like somebody went mad, mad in the medieval way of mad. They didn't become like, oh, demon possessed. No. Somebody got bullied and bullied and bullied and bullied and the grownups did nothing, or the grownups took part in the bullying until one day they break, or they start pulling in evil, reading certain books, listening, and then they decide that all the bullies should die.

You notice how everybody doesn't get shot up at the school and sometimes the school shooter will literally protect other people from them because they are not stark raving mad they fed up, or nobody protected them, so they shoot willy-nilly but they'll lock their favorite teacher in a room instead of shooting them and then go shoot up the rest of the school because they don't want the teacher to be able to call the police and tell but they don't want to shoot that one person. So, if you go through school shootings like a profiler, you'll figure out bullies made the shooter and cowards made the shooter from not stopping the bullies. In my subconscious mind software book when I was a little kid, both of my parents loved the wild west and so I was raised watching cowboy movies. Thus to me there are only Heroes and Villains. And good citizens.

Now, you had to go to a special channel cause it wasn't a regular channel, but you went to like the old movie channel and it was like wild west and Technicolor musicals, which are always joy and happiness and this story works out. Well, I learned really quick a hero versus a villain, but then I would always ask just like Jesus hanging from the cross mom, why are people, such cowards? Daddy, why didn't people help Jesus? Why don't people help the victims in a wild west movie when there's only one villain in town and he has a handful of boys to back him up and the town outnumbers them. Okay. So, we do a class, and it only happens once or twice a year and I open it and you can come and then we close the enrollment just to accommodate the number of people that need to be there. Now we have online, we can take more people, but it's this villain who was here when we rode into town because how come we have so many people allowing bullies because they don't want to take the hit.

The town person that stands up to the bully, cowards harms them, beats them, kills them, they hurt their family. So, they learn just like with cruelty based on class restrictions, those who helped the slaves, they would take those white people who helped and nail them into their houses. Meaning go to their house nail all the windows and doors shut with them inside then set it on fire, have them burn alive, screaming because they're burning alive. Can't get out because all the windows and doors are nailed shut, and then make sure all the neighbors watched. Then they would tell the neighbors if you help them that are currently being burned alive you're next. We'll do that to you right now and if you help any other slaves ever in your life, this is what's going to happen to you. Remember demonic, evil energy that's what racism is. Change the mental commentary.

So, if you're mean, just know that. If you're sitting in church judging witches for calling demons and doing spells. If you're a person full of cruelty, overt conscious permissions to break the law, steal, you've got demons, you are demons and you call them because that's what that energy is. That's what that energy is. That's what it means when it runs through your body. That's what it means. Vibrationally that's what it is. That's why I can call people. There are what: 70 different magical communities in the world. In America, our constitution says people have the right to do what worship they want, and some people have taken that like to the extreme religiously. So, we have 70 different magical communities who don't usually communicate with each other. We really have 40, but some of those have offshoots and so it's 70 different identifiable populations, beliefs and behaviors. But what they all will tell you is understanding energy and then just use different words, light, dark, low, high, creative, destructive, chaos . It's not about being in a world of duality.

Like Buddha said, be the uncarved stone. Don't be yin, don't be yang. Don't even be the yin-yang symbol... Be light with a little bit of dark and dark with a little bit of light No, no, no, no, no, no. That's not balanced. If you had read the book, instead of listening to the stereotypes, you would know the next step to that is the uncarved stone. You are balanced. You're not light with a little dark. You're not dark with a little light. You are balanced. So, in this next chapter, we're going to talk about the two extremes of the balance and how sometimes we don't understand how vicious the subtle evils are and you can say if they're vicious, how can they be subtle? Because they're not the ones that make the news, but they're the ones that make the world go around the evil parts. They're the everyday, all-day little bits of racism. They make stuff like hood rats. It's the constant racial permissions each human has unless you grew up like me where you're not taught any racism. So, I didn't let any cruelty based on class restrictions stick. Even though I learned about it in college, I didn't become angry and become racist against racism. I was like I'm staying soul but I'm going to do some compliance review training for some places that may not understand what sexism or cruelty based on class restrictions is.

A lot of times companies get in trouble (another word for out of compliance) and it's because men are talking to women or men in sexual ways and laughing about it and not getting in trouble. So, they'll get maybe a sexual harassment lawsuit and lose millions of dollars and then they'll get a fine from our federal government for violating federal law because sexual harassment is against federal law, just like cruelty based on class restrictions is against federal law. cruelty based on class restrictions against most state laws and local laws and city laws too. That's why they have the term hate crime. So, I went to a company to do a training for them, compliance review training, which means, hey, we have to show the federal government and the state government that we're not trying to sexually harass women and make them quit their jobs and make them work in an illegal, hostile environment. So, please help us understand how we created this culture without us having to admit more liability, so we don't lose more lawsuits.

I only go to the ones that are really trying to change the environment. So, I go, and I change the subconscious of the humans, which thereby changes the environment.

So, one example that men will ask, because if you've had subconscious permission just like racism to harm with no recourse, sometimes you're attached to, there's nothing wrong with that because you don't get in trouble for it, and we get in trouble for things that are wrong. So, we get this warped evil level of permissions where even if it was wrong, if somebody did it to you personally, because society says you don't get in trouble for it, it becomes less of wrong to your subconscious.

So, guys will say, well, how come we can't talk to them like that? We didn't touch them. Remember energy. Words are energy. The fear you put, the disgust you put, some sexual stuff that you say to somebody who's not attracted to you is literally disgusting to them and disgust works on your digestive system.

You can test and see the change in the health of the digestion system's organs if they're subjected to that because they've been disgusted. Some of them even develop illnesses that can't be diagnosed, where they just vomit constantly. That's because you disgust them with your sexual harassment. That's how much words are energy?

So, finally, I realized one day, instead of taking each man's comments where women were attacking men and repeating this stuff and calling them vile and calling men harmful names. I was like, did you not just hear this man say, this whole world said he can do this, and he likes you. So, he figured you didn't like him back, so he did this because he didn't care if it hurt your feelings because you hurt his feelings.

So, this boils down to what is sexual harassment and everybody got quiet. So, I said, good now this is where I come in for the kill and reprogram the brain.

So, now we access the bad programming. We access the programming that's hurting or is hindering or is holding people back. So, we took that programming out with that discussion. I said

 sexual harassment depends on who says it. It literally boils down to whether or not you like the person. If you're a shy girl and a sexy fireman says stuff to you and you think he's cute, but you could never get him because you're nerdy or you're ugly or he's so far out of your league, you would never get a guy like that. Those same phrases used for sexual harassment are a compliment. Now reverse that and it's your boss and he's unattractive in every way that men define being unattractive. Some people think bald men are sexy, but balding men, most men wouldn't want to be balding. That's why they either shave their head and be full-on sexy bald, or they get hair implants, but they don't like that in-between phase of balding. Maybe they're fat or maybe they're not handsome in the phase or maybe they're too short. Whatever it is that would make you not be attracted to someone, all it takes is one or two of those attractive traits missing and they flirt, and you feel like you are sexually harassed because you're not attracted, and you would never be with them.

know, we're not like that and I will say it to him. A guy I don't like who is my boss taps me on my butt I would still say something. Personally. it's my personality. I would say, please don't do that again. Don't do that again. I don't feel that way. I would make sure I used phrases that included me, not him so that he doesn't become more aggressive or go to ego. I would make it first clear between the two of us do not ever do that again. That's not how I feel. But if they continue to do it, then I would see them as a villain, and you know how I feel about villains.

Now don't get me wrong with my non-judgment being good for your Soul, because when it comes to behaviors we all believe different levels for what is wrong. racism, you'd be amazed how many people who have other racisms have helped me or stopped racists who were committing crimes.

There were police officers in one town. It actually happened in two towns but the first place I started was in one particular town where Police were going to the ghetto area where people lived on section eight and then they would call section eight. The police would call section eight and lie, make up violations to get those people kicked off section eight so that they would lose their homes, lose their housing, lose their ability to have housing at all on this planet. That's why section eight exists so that they have a rent price they can afford. I don't really know how it works, but I know those things. I think there are only two things I know about it of what it is. It's a program that makes rent a lower rate for the person who's living there while the landlord still gets paid their going rate by a government. So, the landlord gets paid the rate they would charge anybody, but the person paying them pays what they can afford. Okay.

That's what I know. But I also knew, could prove, and had evidence and was asked to profile by a famous nonprofit lawyer agency ACLU for protecting the rights of all races of people for things that are happening to the poor and they don't have the money to hire lawyers to handle it. So, they asked me to come back from Paris because I lived in Paris for 10 years and I would go back and forth, to make sure I never violated the law, get my passport stamped. Come back to the US when I was supposed to, go back to Paris when I was allowed, things like that. So, they asked me to make a special trip to come back from Paris, to testify against these police with the evidence that I gave as a profiler. I documented it so well that they didn't need me present, but I realized as a woman, it would help more because it wouldn't just be a lawyer talking to a jury. It would be the traditional female gender roles saying how much this is hurting people. Not just, these are laws that were violated and the evil intent of the officer's doing it. Do you know why those officers were doing that? People were getting killed in that city.

So, the police could have been there to stop those murders as opposed to murdering people's hope, making children homeless, making old people homeless, making single women who chose to work as a secretary instead of somewhere else that may have harmed her Soul more to be able to afford to have a place to live. So, evil had Police officers breaking the law and they were doing evil things. Now I don't want you to start thinking even that is a judgment because people like that when the courts don't get them evil people do, so there are evil people that will help stop other evil people or evil will step in and take out someone who's doing evil things based on who's trying to stop them or to support me or to support you.

So, consciousness has a lot of other faces than the ones we're used to seeing. It has its everyday actions. When I say, oh my waitress made a mistake, or the waitress did this or that. One time I was with my sorority sisters and we were sitting, we were at a convention, we had a little bit of time for lunch, you know, probably like an hour and a half. But with that many people all trying to have lunch at the same time, that's a lot for food service staff to prepare for. So, we didn't want pre-prepared food we wanted restaurant food.

So, we went to a restaurant and the waitress just because they were being racist, and we were all in suits and we were chatting and talking to each other. I always say, no one should have to serve me and my sorority sisters, because we all know each other as sorority sisters, but we don't all know each other really, really tight as women but we all know ourselves really, really well. So, you don't get I'll have the steak and potatoes. You don't get I'll have the shrimp salad. That's not how we order. We know ourselves and what we like and don't like, so well that we say, I'll have the lobster bisque and a lobster tail. I would like a little more butter added to the lobster bisque and I would like to have melted, not clarified butter with the lobster tail. I would like a 7-Up with no ice and a Perrier water so I can water down the seven up to cut the sugar. That's one person's order. These people get so mad. You don't even have the right to be breathing. How dare you have the right to think you deserve some luxury. How dare you have the right to order in a way I don't even know how to order, and I've been working at a restaurant forever because we're raised at much better restaurants. But when we order it can be any kind of little mom and pop. It could be a chain that is known for cheap, quick food but calling themselves a restaurant kind of like a Denny's.

We'll go into Denny's because they were open after we are finishing something for charity, and we'll still order like we're at some expensive, posh restaurant and our qualifications of what we want to come with our meal. When I order a hamburger, I want it medium rare with A1 steak sauce and if they don't have A1 steak sauce, I don't want other steak sauce. I'll just take salt and pepper with some soy sauce. So, some people, if they're really, really hateful in their hearts and racist, they don't want you to have had an education or a life that you can say anything more than I'll take this and point to the number. You ever notice how, in some restaurants where you're experiencing an Asian person who is racist because not all Asian people are racist, but you're experiencing one who is and while you're reading the menu, they tell you just pick the number. You don't have to know how to read it, which

I find funny sometimes, because when you think about it, I can read very well. This is coming from somebody who probably can't, the person who's saying it to me or a restaurant owner who will rush over and apologize and be like, she's coming here since she was a child, she knows exactly what she wants, and she doesn't need the number. The owner says explaining to the waitress about me. Its incredible how the mind of the waitress could not see me only her unenlightened concepts.

Then they'll say something to them about their level of speaking English or not. But measuring people's worth based on how well they speak English is a part of the under surface classism energy , that cruelty based on class restrictions in truth is what? Classism, because no matter or what race somebody is the manner in which they speak English has gateways for them. Behaviors, ways people think they can treat them or mistreated them based on how they speak English with an accent without an accent and I mean a Southern accent.

The vocabulary used. Sometimes people have malaprops. That means, they mean to say the Pacific Ocean but instead, they say "specific ocean" because they don't understand the big words that they use and so they use a word that sounds like the word they meant. Used by Shakespeare even has a character called Mrs Malaprop in 1700s play by Brinsley Sheridan because when you are of a certain educational level and you don't know a large vocabulary, sometimes that means physical words that are really long you only have heard not read so the brain chooses another word "it does know" so those persons never know other times, it means the number of words you have available for use. ism because it's built on classism likes to make sure that when the poor are poorly educated, they are uneducated meaning the vocabulary they have access to from kindergarten through their senior year of high school is less than 10% not even a quarter most researchers assume they know, let alone half of what a well-educated person would have. They want to restrict their vocabulary. That's why they love if you use slang because it makes you think you have a larger vocabulary than you do, and it also makes you highly identifiable anywhere but where they want you to be.

So, if you go somewhere, the word you use to ask them, even of how much is this dress? Whether or not you call it a dress or a gown or a tea dress or a ball gown or a day dress, if you just say dress it says something to them, more than if you identify the type of dress, but also the words you use to say how much. So, I've traveled all around the world, and when I travel, I always make sure I know five words in the language where I am visiting: please, thank you, how much. How much does this cost? How much is it? So, in Italy quanto costa. How much? Hi, goodbye. Okay. Hello, and goodbye says kindness, thank you gratitude. Those are all uplifting. You matter so I'm saying hi. I'm not just walking up and saying, how much is this? I say, thank you. Thank you for your time. Thank you for being part of my life for these moments. Thank you for having met you once again, increasing the vibe. Sometimes I say my name, sometimes I ask their name, but then I ask how much, and I know my vocabulary is huge and sometimes another part of racism where people of a lower social position will correct what you're saying based on their lower class saying they're your better and they don't understand WHAT you are saying so you must be saying something else and that person will be wrong in correcting what you're saying. No, I chose the word. I meant. That's what I meant. It's just that you're asking for something or you're asking them to do something, and they don't understand all the words you're using, and their cruelty based on class restrictions tells them instead of them not having an education and making a mistake that you must have made the mistake because they've never heard of that word. Because they haven't heard of that word and they're racist, that word must not exist because their racism tells them you would never know words they don't know. So, you must be so silly that you made up a word.

So, they figure out a word they think you meant and tell you that's what you must've meant. See why there's a nice way to talk about cruelty based on class restrictions because the real big, bad wolf in racism is not the billboards we see happening. It's all these little bits of evil and nuance separating souls, separating humans into little hate groups instead of communicating a soul and recognizing soul that person's soul, your soul, and the bodies belong to Soul. Soul doesn't belong to your personality, your ego, or your body.

Prolog

You are the human flesh costume that God gave Soul this lifetime to experience this world, to try to learn the stuff in this book and some stuff and other people's books, and to unlearn the programming from television. Now I love TV so I'm not saying don't watch TV. That's even programming where people don't watch TV and then they think they're better than everyone else because they don't watch TV. They still have the same negative programming. It's just coming from different sources, including thinking they're better than other people because they don't watch TV. That's a programming kind of like vegetarians they think they're better than meat-eaters. I was a vegetarian for 28 years. At no point was I willing to lose my level of consciousness by judging and thinking that meant I was better than people who ate meat just like there are people who are vegetarians, who don't even know why they're vegetarians other than is politically correct, but we'll talk about why it can be spiritually correct, and we'll talk about what happens when you grow. The LORD will shatter your enemies.

Now the last racism I want us to talk about in this little tea party of ours is when people use cruelty based on class restrictions in your head to manipulate you. I was in a meeting that was supposed to be a mediation. Someone stole almost $200,000 from me; Tony and Jennifer Cheung stole my inventory because they thought they could and that there'd be no criminal charges against them based on their racism. 1st they Defrauded me and had me pay them for a five-year lease for a building that didn't exist after they 2nd said was because they were racist against white people and said that. Then after 3rd committing those two crimes committed so many other crimes, Extortion, including trying to have people spiritually use negative intent. 4th I shouldn't say trying to have, paying people to spiritually attack to try to ruin finances, happiness blessings all because they committed criminal acts of fraud and theft, extortion including going into my office and my home, making keys and giving the keys to other people so 14 people could go in and steal what they wanted based on the arrogance, "racism allows us to do whatever we want".

So, we're going to do this because we're now exposed for the fraud and the real estate for your office, with the five-year lease for a place that didn't exist. So, they made a lot of racial slurs about white people. They made racial slurs about black people. They may racial slurs about Mexican people and they decided that they could do all of this based on that racism and that said "no one would stop them". There would be no one who physically stopped them. There would be no one who legally stopped them. So, they started doing a whole bunch of black magic to try to make those things happen. So, anyone they encountered that they wanted to manipulate, they would try to use the person's racism, meaning the stereotypes that existed in that person's head they would come into agreement with that. So, pull it up, find it in the people's heads, pull it up, and then play on it meaning, oh, well, you know, these people always exaggerate, or people like them. So, now you have someone who's supposed to be arresting them, fining them, making them have to pay the money they stole or owe and them using the subconscious and conscious racist permissions in that person's head while mumbling words for energetic manipulations.

So, there was a woman named Darshan. Now her name is Norma so the person who names their child, Norma only maybe to honor the name of someone else, like maybe one grandmother was named Norma and then were hippies and so they wanted to name their child Darshan, but they named her Norma to honor their mother or their grandmother because names not usually that level of difference. The hippie-dippy or the yoga girl renaming themselves something like Darshan or the hippie spiritualists naming themselves. So, most likely it was not her birth name, may or may not be your birth name based on socials meaning sociological reasons that a profiler would come up with. So, this person was supposed to be impartial, but this person's sentences started with people like you. Vocabulary always shows that were different levels and different types of racist are present.

Now, when people start talking to a profiler with a sentence like people like you, I try to help them understand they're being racist by pointing things out in their head without saying it. So, you just say something back like, like me. I would go: people with red hair? because I have natural red hair and so I'll say something like that. I want them to understand what they've just said and they'll either say, I didn't say that, (conscious) or did I say that?(subconscious revealed) because their subconscious is telling on them while they're in your face pretending to be unbiased.

    a. They cancelled the Mediation we had scheduled for months. So, they're in your face as a neutral party, but they're so full of stereotypes and cruelty based on class restrictions in their head they don't have the ability to be impartial because impartiality is not in their personal makeup. Meaning they're so racist, they're so classist, they're so prejudiced in what they think.

b. They break basic protocols usually required because they don't apply to the poor. They figure you can't afford a lawyer so they violate your legal protections.

Not everything is racism. We can't be silly. Racism means you're putting one race above another, or you're thinking something about an entire race that determines how you treat everyone in that race. Prejudice is if you think all Chinese people eat rice, okay. That's prejudice because of course, it's never all of anybody. Somewhere there's a Chinese person who doesn't eat rice. So, that as a blatant thing, we might all think on a subconscious level as a prejudice, we would not assign a wrong or cruel treatment by us that is okay based on that prejudice. Okay. So, prejudice doesn't usually come with action and especially prejudice doesn't usually come with a permissioned action. So, the rest of the world mistreats this race of people. Okay. So, if you say black people, Mexican people, poor white people, you would...

They decide the law applies to you but it does not apply to them, thus they are quoting the law to you while they are breaking it the law does not apply to them. In some cases they apply the law to you extra. And then they break them.

So, as we now know, if you didn't know before, a lot of people have prejudice. Most prejudices are things we think we know about somebody. Very often somebody will say something to you, or somebody has actually... I'll use another example. Someone once said to me, this is brie and I mean, slowly, they said this slowly, slowly while pointing to the Brie. This - is -Brie. It - is - cheese. Slow like a robot running out of battery and I was just like, I don't know why this person thinks, I wouldn't know that that cheese called Brie. But instead of going there and being insulted by some prejudice that exists in some racist heads, because saying it to me, means not just do you think it, but you're going to act on it and come over to me and speaking so slowly means that you somehow think that I need you to explain something I haven't asked.

That's always a sign of really rampant racism. When someone explains something to you that you do understand that they assume you don't understand out of prejudices in their head, they're being racist. They're basically walking over to you and saying, I know you're beneath me and you don't know basic things about the world so I'm going to make myself feel better and pull a false sense of superiority and explain something basic to you because you're such an inferior creature.

That's what Norma Darshan took part in she lead a meeting. Norma Darshan Brach was supposed to be impartial but broke the law and constantly spouted her personal privileges .

Now some people will do it in a normal voice, and they really just have prejudice, and they think you don't understand because of the prejudice in their head about your race, sexual preference, genders or your social class. But if they explain it condescendingly, their self-esteem is attached to being better than you thereby exposing them to be the insecure sexist /racist that they are.

So, their purpose in life: the only way they feel good about themselves in life is feeling better that they are better than you or you are less than them. Got it. That's what makes them feel like they are somebody. Not being somebody, not being kind, not making the world different just every person of your race is beneath them. That's what makes them feel good about themselves?

So, Norma Darshan Brach was one of these people, Brach like the candy, first name Norma.

Norma Darshan Brach, B-R-A-C-H like the candy, but behavior not sweet. First name Norma, N-O-R-M-A and Then Darshan like when spiritual people think or feel they have spiritual enlightenment. She was one of these people. Darshan is spelled D-A-R-S-H-A-N. She doesn't work for UC Berkeley, but she's a sometimes lectures for the School of Law at UC Berkeley. But she's a lawyer who was so racist that in a mediation process, she allowed the Meditation scheduled for months to be cancelled replaced it without telling Plaintiff with a meeting held by the defense.

There were 3 parties just making racism and was racist to one of the parties. She was so incredibly racist that she allowed the defendant to be racist and then took part in things. When you're in mediation, all parties sign a piece of paper to say, hey, we're going to participate in mediation. This is who I am. These are the rules for mediation and then please sign the paper and have confidentiality.

Well, she canceled that meeting with the defense only. This is how biased permissions work. The law doesn't matter even when you're a lawyer. She canceled the time and place of that meeting, had the defendant host the meeting, waited for the plaintiff to arrive at the scheduled meeting then said we cancelled the mediation And Wakako is going to hold a meeting so the defendants are the people being sued for doing a wrong. The plaintiff is the victim that they stole from, whatever reason they're being sued. Have the plaintiff show up for the other meeting that had been scheduled and by the agreement signed and then had somebody waiting there to say this meeting's been canceled. Not a phone call, not an email, nothing. Not a discussion, nothing to say the meeting you've waited for over a month is not taking place in a legal manner. We're going to do this little racist ambush but passive-aggressively, you know how like so many are totally passive-aggressive.

So, this kind of behavior. So, either she goes by Darshan Norma Brach, or she goes by Norma Darshan Brach So, this woman is a licensed attorney in the state of California. According to UC Berkeley, she lectures there maybe one or two times a year. She tries to pull the world's craziest racist powerplay ever, and not doing what UC Berkeley policy, business courtesy protocol, basic Mediation business would be.

People when as a group has discussed they can harm without recourse (without anyone else knowing) those people like Darshan and Wakako Unritani together and separately knowing and licensed to follow protocols planned to violate them: The meditation is canceled- would have been a simple message, or the mediation and meeting is rescheduled via email or phone call. She doesn't do that. Instead, why not do something sneaky and underhanded like let the defendants hold a different meeting. Now with mediation, the defendants aren't supposed to hold it, the mediators are supposed to hold it. That's the purpose of having a mediator, to be in a neutral place with an unbiased uninterested party. But racism, especially subconscious cruelty based on class restrictions combined with conscious blatant cruelty based on class restrictions, sprinkled, and seasoned with subconscious prejudices means you can do this kind of stuff to certain races of people because how will they know any better and also what's going to happen to you if you did. Nothing.

So, that's how their brain is thinking when they do it. So, we'll proceed into the meeting.

So, the plaintiff, so I go to the place it's been scheduled. There's one girl there and her purpose of being there is to tell me the mediation has been moved. Once that takes place, then the defendant who's been doing all kinds of stuff. Black people are monkeys according to her clients so they can do whatever they want. I mean, they just do all kinds of craziness. Wakako Uritani a lawyer that lies to judges. Doesn't serve documents. Wakako She has lied on judges. She has told one judge another judge said something and not only did that judge not say it. She never even spoke to the judge. Meaning Wakako lied and told one judge A that she had a long conversation with another judge B and then gave a full report of the conversation that she never had to another judge C to lie and make the judge C she was giving the verbal account to that everything she wanted was agreed to by another judge B- it was just she never even met the judge B she pretended the statement by a judge she has never met or spoken to.

conversation Now, you know, they're supposed to pull your law license if you're a lawyer going around lying on judges and lying to judges and lying in paperwork. They're are just so crooked, so evil but she's extremely arrogant. So, she feels that because of the country's cruelty based on class restrictions, no one will stop her from doing the illegal stuff she's doing in all her cases and her name is Wakako Uritani. I'll spell that out in a minute, that kind of thing.

But her name is Wakako Uritani and she, for 18 months filed papers that normally the plaintiff would file and pretend that the plaintiffs filed it when the judge would ask about it. So, the judge would think that it was the plaintiff's idea to go to the mediation. I mean, it was just so much wrong, crazy stuff that she was doing on so many levels. She is so evil that friends I have, see her in their meditations in 6 different places around the world and will call out of the blue and say, who is this woman attacking you? Who is this woman doing all this stuff? The nuns, it's so funny that Buddhist nuns, they will say, oh my goodness, she's crazy, talking about Wakako. They'll look at her picture and to them, she's just a demon. So, they squint their eyes and look away because they say they don't want to look upon evil. They spend their time there praying all day, they're Buddhists. So they said they'd have to get their Master for such an evil crazy woman as Uritani Wakako.

So, they, Nuns say dear oh, she's crazy and then the other one said, no, she's evil and crazy. We must go get our master. We need our master's help for her. Right. So, these are nuns of like

20, 30, and 40 years. Three nuns, one. So, they start just praying, give little glass necklaces for prayer because Wakako is so evil and she's an attorney and she's too weak to win without breaking 600 laws of court rules. So, she's just trying to make a mess and manipulate and confuse people. That's her thing. That's what she does. So, this person, Norma Darshan Brach is supposed to be a mediator who then falls into this classist pattern of they're lawyers and so they get to do what they want. So, they're going to twist the law, which means break the law and do this stuff that I wouldn't be able to tell anybody that they did it.

But what they did was they had people present at that meeting who didn't sign the paper to be at the meeting and who were not noted to the plaintiff, which means they didn't say to me or anyone else that that person would be at the meeting. Then they had some people present by phone with private images. It was really, really all out of the ordinary, but all so racist and blatant based on what they were trying to do. Now, I didn't say this before, but they were under court order to have this mediation for settlement. Not to play games, not to be racist, not to be silly, not to make a joke out of the

US justice system, and not to violate what a judge, a sitting California State judge told them to do.

They figured the judge would think the mediation was just not successful as opposed to the mediation was sabotaged so that it would not produce the settlement that they're under court order to come up with. So, they let the defendant host a meeting via Zoom through Wakako account. Now anyone that's holding Zoom meetings in 2021 knows that a lot of meetings are taking place by Zoom now, but you also know that Zoom can have breakout sessions and rooms. You send certain participants to certain rooms and then they have a private discussion but everybody's in the meeting on the same Zoom all at once. It also means that they put her in charge of who she could drop from the meeting who the meeting would accept and dismiss, who could be heard and who could not be heard, who could write, who could not write. This was a meeting held instead of the mediation.

So, Wakako was playing with all of these controls and the mediators were all plugged into their prejudices or racism. So, they were supposed to hold the meeting. They should have been in control of who can talk and who can't talk. So, there were times where things were said, and I couldn't hear anybody because Wakako blocked it. There were times where I was dropped by Wakako from the meeting and would have to call back and wait to be put in. Then the mediators' racism, once prejudices are agreed on, they're like an invisible, energetic handshake. What that means is the energetic handshake is their subconscious are in agreement.

When we look scientifically, energetically most know someone who feels we all think the same about certain races of people or certain classes of people. So, that person uses the things "we" think. they don't know because society is set up for them not to know the truth is we are all Soul.

So, the mediators should have hosted the scheduled mediation instead of cancelling it. Then the mediators, should not have attended a meeting held by Wakako at the same time scheduled for the mediation.

It was not a mistake. If someone else needed to host it, we should have gotten together as a group and decided how that was going to take place. Once that part took place, we should have then had the person hosting, the main person, the person who was in control of the controls have cohosts, who are also in control of the controls. The people who should have also been in control of who could talk, who could hear, when people spoke, breakout rooms, and breakout sessions, should have been the mediators. So, they should have been the host s and if nothing else, they should have been the cohosts able to do that. They didn't do that either.

So when someone has an evil personality, One of their first tactics is recruitment Define evil or painting you and use that get the evil they want done using your soul and your life force.

evil They just let Wakako do it. So, she was doing what she'd been doing since the defendants got sued for their crimes of fraud and extortion and actual theft and threats and physical attacks of Plaintiff.

So, as the meeting went on, the conversations that they've had separately wherein Wakako Uritani plugged in. Uritani is U-R-I-T-A-N-I, plugged in, and using their racism. So, they became a team, the unbiased parties supposed to mediate are now a team out of racism with the defense. So, their way to handle it, their comments exposing the discussion they had about their prejudices, and their level of racism start to come out in their comments. So, Darshan Brach is saying you know, Norma is saying things like people like you to me. Wakako,

W-A-K-A-K-O, Wakako like some anime villain in Vampire Knight is pushing the buttons. So, sometimes I can't hear what people are saying, or people are expecting me to talk but they can't hear. The person that they had from another company unannounced company. Her name was Tracy Jowers, and she wasn't there to assure anything. She couldn't hear what I said because Wakako would turn me down or kick me out of the meeting. So, people would think that's all that was said, or I wouldn't be able to say anything, and it was not a meeting in which I spoke than a few minutes, although the meeting lasted for hours, because not only did they not make the breakout rooms and the breakout sessions. They held most of the meeting without me just calling me on my cell phone three or four times well they staying in a meeting Wakako and someone claiming to be Cheung.

So, a mediation person would be the mediator. The defendants sit in one room, the plaintiffs sit in another room. The mediator goes back and forth between those two physical rooms, negotiating a settlement for the $193,000 that they stole not to mention the other damages they caused, but just for that much $220,000 -225,000.00 So, in the Zoom meeting, what you do is kind of like when we're having our workshops and our meetings, then you break out for team sessions. It's just like any conference where you break out for team sessions. You're still in the same meeting and then what's private goes into a breakout room and the room is numbered and you can see the attendees and the host can see it all and the host can go in it all. So, the host can go into any room and the two people are supposed to be in separate rooms, but they let Wakako be the host. So, now there's no rooms and it's them talking to Wakako on a private call doing all of their stuff together.

This is supposed to be the impartial mediator and then I'm just not even on a Zoom, one on no call and you can see because what they would do is call me on my cell phone for two or three minutes and they said, well, Wakako said to tell you, and it would be something like Wakako said to tell you, don't tell their insurance what they did, something like that. Then they would leave and go back and hang out for another 20, 30 minutes. While I stood at the beach waiting for my cell phone to ring.

But you can always tell based on the semantics, based on vocabulary, what someone is doing or not doing. So, based on Darshan's verbiage to me, Ali's (Ah-lee) verbiage to me, and

Emily's verbiage to me they were having racist and prejudice discussion with Wakako for long periods of time and a mediator, an unbiased vocabulary is defendant's attorney plaintiff's attorney, or you say, Miss Uritani, Dr. Morgan White.

That's the vocabulary you use because they're trying to stay professionally distant. So as a profiler, you can tell in how someone addresses (you can check the intimacy) kind of like women If you have a friend or somebody at church or somebody at your office or your husband's office, you always know if your husband's having an affair with that woman, based on the word, based on the vocabulary of familiarity is what it's called. So, when you're too buddy-buddy, with somebody you just met. So, in this case, business stuff, they're only locking in on commonality. They're not old buddies. It's a common filter, common prejudices in their head, common filter. You know that woman is having an affair with your husband at his office because she doesn't call your husband her position in the company. If she calls him Bob, or if she calls him Mr. Williams in a certain way, you know good and well, that energy is too familiar for people professionally distancing themselves. So, professional distance is a vocabulary we choose on purpose to say, she's this on a business level, or to say, I'm not on your team or their team.

So it's like that old joke about three men walk into a bar that what happens is when people have their subconscious in-check and then if they walk into a room where everybody else who should also have their Evil in-check instead has it out in the open (when the cats away...) and they bring evil acts that makes them feel powerful out in the open and then they do it together when this happens in meetings that are supposed to be confidential they think their victim won't be able to tell what they did because of the confidentiality --- so then like a pack they do more and more and more that they would normally hide; thinking no one will ever know what they did and every time they feel like no one's going to know the more horrible things they do.

So, they didn't do any negotiation. The meeting was not our mediation. It was a meeting Wakako somehow talked them into doing because our mediation was canceled and didn't take place. Then they had a meeting where Wakako hosted in Zoom but didn't make them hosts and they didn't insist on it which they should have as mediators or canceled until we could have the meeting. There was never a justifiable reason why they didn't have the meeting that had been scheduled for a month and a half, nor why they didn't email to cancel it or reschedule it or a phone call to cancel or reschedule it because it was all a kind of protocol set up. You'll see this very often in corruption.

So, as a profiler, you can follow historical patterns of corruption to undo crimes that people thought no one would be able to explain.

So, Norma Darshan Brach or Darshan Norma Brach, depending on how she feels like writing her name. She thought this protocol and their antics would be protected by the fact that you're not supposed to talk about what happens in mediation. The mediators are supposed to be private and respect privacy. The people that took part, you come up with a settlement, they pay the settlement. But Brach didn't hold her mediation. But after they pulled all this stuff, she kept saying, you can't tell anybody what we did because mediations are private. You can't even tell the judge what we did and would be bragging about it as if they came up with this plan to waste time for the court, not to be able to know they did this and for it to seem like Wakako and Tony and Jennifer Cheung complied with the court's order, as opposed to being held in contempt of court for violating the court's order.

So, they violated the court's order, but a fake meeting was going to help them, and the plotting in their heads is what made them glue together as a group so that they said very racist and prejudicial comments and had someone not noticed, someone else not supposed to be in the meeting, in the meeting and in and out of the meeting and then left the meeting without notice while I wasn't included in that. So, it was me standing somewhere for more than two hours with my cell phone, every 25 to 40 minutes, getting a phone call from one of the mediators or two of the mediators with a comment that was also inappropriate. Then they would get off the phone and go back and hang out with Wakako for a little while and they thought they could present this as following the court orders to come up with a settlement.

So, someone who owes you $193,000, who wastes that much time and violates the court order and said, you take the $1,000 they're offering one thousand dollars. They owe you 193,000 they just wanted to be able to tell the court they weren't able to come up with the settlement, which was what they wanted in the first place because they didn't like the court's order that we had to go to mediation ALTHOUGH they asked the court to order to mediation 2 years ago when they were trying to avoid going to trial. That's how crazy and evil, just like the nuns said Wakako is evil and crazy. So, she wanted the mediation so she could keep her clients' deeds from a jury. Wakako pretended for 2 years like no one was participating, but she did that for a year and a half then the court decided, why is this taking so long? You asked for this, why aren't you doing it? I was like, your honor, I didn't ask for this Wakako just made it seem like I asked for this. Wakako asked for it. The defendants asked for it to stop us from going to trial.

When someone is evil they like to play with People's heads. Of course, HOW WAS THE JUDGE SUPPOSED TO KNOW, that's not normal way because the defense doesn't usually ask for mediation, the plaintiff asks for it. So, then he's like, okay, so here's the court order: You guys go get this settled.

So Evil Was Afoot when we went to see the mediator:

So, what it means to be a mediator, they violated that. What it means to be a lawyer in the state of California, they violated that. Following the court order, they violated that. Who's in a mediation who's allowed in the meeting, who's not. What does the paperwork look like? How meetings take place? None of us were assigned to be in a meeting, held by Wakako for her demonic antics but their evil subconscious said they would try to use every loophole and every stereotype and the stereotypes where the plaintiff won't understand. The plaintiff doesn't have the brainpower or the education to understand. They kept expressing that and by using people like you, you people because when someone doesn't quantify who the you people are, the you people are always some prejudice in their head. They don't say you people to tall people, but I will joke if somebody is being really rude, I literally will joke and say, oh, do you mean tall people? Got it.

I will say, oh, because I'm so tall. Because people who say you people have subconscious permission beyond social norms and protocols. I once had a student call another student at the N-word. That's not the only time it happened but one time when it happened, I gave him detention and I called his mother. His mother came to school and instead of like my other student whose dad was like, what the heck is wrong with you? Where'd you get that from? We're not like that. So, he's speaking to his child revealing his own subconscious (we as people don't do what some other people that look like us do. Don't do this) meaning his Dad had taught him better.

Now, take my other student, his mom came to school and what she said is "I told you not to talk like that in front of people". So, this household did use the N-word, did talk very racist stuff about black people, Mexican people, Chinese people all the time. But she taught her children when they're around "other" don't say it.

That's our last type of racism for this class, this book, this tea party. Alice went to court too. But you know how I am. We can have discussions, we'll have one-on-ones, and we'll have some meet and greets for when Evil is trying to undo you as Soul, how you can deal with that, or all ism that you grew up with- that you don't want to keep, how you get that Evil dust out of you and how you get to be you, your authentic self without Wakako and people like her can't find a way in. I don't mean that in the passive-aggressive girls, fake authentic self. I mean, if you don't like something about yourself, how do you get a new gumball and energetically make that a real thing. Be A True You.

Scream the loudest. Ali =(AH-lee)(the Frog Footman)

So, when someone is being racist, like that group was being some manipulated, some happy that, ooh, the gang's all here. Kind of like, ooh, I don't have to keep my racism quiet because I'm in good racist company. You don't scream. You don't yell, you don't react. You let them keep showing their pattern and then you speak up like me in a way that it helps everybody and scream the loudest with a pen. When people who are normally racist towards a person stops and lets that person be racist with them to another group it makes the evil in that person (normally marginalized) feel good.

It was like the racism was that type gets into this weird bacchanal kind of frenzy where the things they keep subconscious are consciously agreed upon to only come out at certain times, meaning there's conscious social permission for when it's okay to act completely racist blatantly with disregard.

So, the bacchanal does not happen just on a conscious level. It happens when the subconscious agrees energetically in a pool. So, now you've got shared subconscious racism in one room together or in one meeting together or in one incident together in which the subconscious which always ran the show, come out in agreement. So, then the energy gives a release for the conscious mind to express things they normally don't express and what is normally settings where it's not safe because racism isn't just about who the races are. There's a heck of black people, racist against black people, Chinese people racist against Chinese people, white people racist against other white people. There's so much but when it comes down to it, if you go with these groups of behaviors for soul that is in this book, you already covered every kind.

This story was inspired by the true-life actions of Tony Cheung and Jennifer Cheung located at 310 7th Street in Oakland, California. They unfortunately tried to teach me the world was only racist, but my parents had already taught me so many wonderful things about Chinese people and Japanese people and Malaysian people and Korean people and Vietnamese people and Taiwanese people and Filipino people that I knew. They weren't representative of all the racism they spouted calling black people monkeys, calling white people names, mocking that they don't have to pay city taxes, state taxes, sale taxes, that they can build without permits. They can build without licensed contractors, that they can lie and connive in every way possible. Try to cheat the justice system, rob, and steal, but think because they were Chinese they would not be arrested. Hire a Chinese man to physically attack me and have to spend 18 months to recover from that attack as they sat and laughed with their racist jokes about white people and black people. How they stole my laptop with 17 books and 18 years of photos taken around the world, more than 100,000 photos taken from all around the world to make my books better, to raise money for charities.

They thought the racism they felt entitled to could stop souls healing. They robbed from every soul who would have come to my office by stealing my equipment. They robbed from every soul who would have walked their road by stealing my artwork, my canvases, my supplies. They stole from every person trying to heal from trauma when they stole my mermaid tails and my mannequins and all the custom fabric and all the years, eight years of saving to buy, to open an apothecary, a healing center, an office, and a loft. They stole from people who needed to tell their stories when they stole the dining table for journaling, antique with carved hand-carved chairs with seashells, chairs worth $500 each. They stole when they stole my shelving, they stole from those souls when they stole my French tart pans. It takes a lot of money to buy 40 French pans.

They stole when they stole 1,000 paintbrushes from 100 paint sets so that people could come in and heal their hearts and minds from rape and attacks and pedophiles. They stole from those souls that are healing. They stole from witches who came to me for therapy. They stole from necromancers who came to me for acceptance. They stole from people who were depressed and suicidal, who couldn't buy those art kits, who couldn't buy those canvases, who couldn't come to classes, who no longer had customer-made jewelry made for them. They stole from the artist who helped me carve those necklaces out of bamboo. They stole from me $193,000 and they did it all out of what they said was their right as Chinese to be racist.

They made up an office with an address that did not exist. They had no building permits. They didn't even have the proper building address. They tried to rewrite history based on lies and stereotypes or constantly demonically gloating about their right to be racist.

What did they always say? Chinese people are more racist than white people. We're just smarter than white people. So, we keep our mouths shut. We're quiet so white people can take the blame and we can get away with more racism. So, they didn't just mean calling black people monkeys or calling Mexicans spics or calling white people trash or stupid. They did all that, but they meant having businesses in the state of California, where they collect thousands of dollars of cash every day and don't pay taxes on it. They meant taking the side of a building on Webster and cutting a hole in it with contractors with no license and no building permits and building. See, a white person couldn't build without building permits without fear of their business being shut down. A white contractor could not work on a building with no license and have a whole work crew in there multiple times without permission from the city without fearing being fined or imprisoned or losing any licensing they had, or the ability to get licensing later, A white person couldn't have done any of the things that they did without being arrested and they bragged that they could do it because of the racist permissions in their conscious mind that were so extreme they felt no need to hide things in their subconscious.

But I will tell you as a doctor, one thing hidden in their subconscious is you don't become that evil when you like yourself. You see in their subconscious must be some self-hate. In their subconscious must be some insecurity. In their subconscious must be some inferiority because they don't need to invoke that much power to harm that many souls to feel like you're powerful. When you're powerful, you're just powerful, like Snow White and Cinderella and the Little Mermaid and Rapunzel. You have power because power flows through you not because of who you crush but because of who you uplift. These people tried to convince me that that was being Chinese as opposed to that was being evil.

But my parents raised me with no racism. They taught me no stereotypes about anyone in the whole world. So, just because they looked a certain way on the outside and hundreds of other Chinese people helped them. There are billions of Chinese people with this hidden racism and when they hired Wakako Uritani they had already bragged about how the white lawyers in the company were going to have to protect them. They even tried to have black people in the company that hired the lawyer to seem that they weren't racist because that lawyer had a black person, But when they weren't filing false papers to the court after I sued them and they weren't lying and Wakako wasn't constantly breaking the law they must've been sleeping because every waking hour since they took my money for a five-year lease and stole my equipment and my laptops, and even went so far as to brag, that all of my things were free to all of Chinatown.

They made keys for men to go in and take whatever they wanted. They even cut a door into the back of a bakery so you can enter from sixth street and Chinatown through a restaurant and go through into my apothecary and to my workshop, into my office, into everything that I owned and steal whatever you want. That's what Tony and Jennifer Cheung did and every soul that is helped by the work that I have done for 27 years and every soul that didn't get help because of their crime and every energetic attack, negative thought, demon. Every single thing they did and every person they hired were seen by Buddhist nuns and Buddhist monks and Baptist preachers and Catholic priests and metaphysicians and yoga girls, and witches who all meditated to see what happened to the place that judges no one and helps everyone.

What happened when I opened the physical place because I'd given my word for eight years, that I promised to build them a place where I would stay put, where they didn't have to come to a conference and fly and get hotels to take a class, where they didn't have to come to an event or an expo or a festival to get a healing or encouragement or books or products created to give them joy and peace and save their lives or the manufactured products created from my art that we sold to stop villains and do documentaries and stop the ills in our world towards women. They didn't care about any of that. They cared about the harm that their subconscious and conscious mind told them they could do, and no one would do anything to them. I don't believe we live in a world like that. I live in a world where they should pay for what they did. I live in a world where villains pay for what they do. They hurt so many magical communities. They hurt so many victims. They hurt me. They even hurt the man that they got to hurt me.

Wakako T. Uritani is an attorney for Lorber law, between them they committed so many crimes in the physical world while constantly sending attacks in the spiritual world, payment is due for all those souls. They owe for all that theft. They owe for stealing the money. They owe for the setup that they built from the start to defraud out of the racism in their head that told them they could. Not the racism I guessed, the racism they said verbally and bragged about and laughed as I, the power company, the cable company, the US Post Office, the city all found out that the place they rented to me, the one they had me pay a five-year lease for didn't exist. They looked for a victim and they based that victim on the race and in their head, the racism in their hearts, the arrogance of their evil.

Wilhelmina Pure Good

We make manga

So, Wakako Uritani broke every law involved in any civil lawsuit. Wakako Uritani broke every law. The way it was explained to me is that she broke every law that you learned the first year of law school to never do and her racism told her that she could violate the court, lie to the judge, lie on the judge, lie on other judges, lie to one judge about another judge. We've only had one judge but between the lies and the spiritual attacks, she never let up. She never stopped her racism and there's a string of paperwork, piles, a flood of paperwork showing how much she violated the law and shouldn't have a law license. Lawyers are supposed to win because they're better not because one lawyer follows the law and the other one breaks it mercilessly.

Then because she knew that even in breaking the law, she kept being exposed for violating the law she paid and pay for spiritual attacks, all witnessed by Buddhist monks and Buddhist nuns and other communities who see the invisible parts of the world.

It's time she paid for what she did. It's time she paid for what she does and now you all know what they thought stays hidden because of their right to abuse white people and black people. That's the way their head works. That's the way Tony Cheung who sits outside of New Tin's Market that store every day at 7th Street and Harrison, in Oakland, California, Chinatown, and Jennifer sits inside and Wakako sits in her office .

They somehow thought our country was a world where all of this was okay, where they attacked victims who came for healing. Wakako attacked witches. Wakako Uritani is an attorney so evil she biologically attacked witches. They owe the Universe so much for the harm they caused and that payment starts this moment and continues for all the souls they robbed, of their classes and products we manufactured for the Souls who have never seen them because Lober, Tony, Jennifjer Wakako wanted to spit on our constitution and and that the payment doesn't stop until those souls are all healed.

Ta Da